The Key to Your Church's Vision

The Practical Guide to Praying For Your Pastor

John Cameron King

Dedication

This book is dedicated to my wife, who has
been faithful to pray for me when no one
else has been aware I needed prayer.

Acknowledgments

I am deeply thankful to the Holy Spirit. He has been my greatest source of inspiration in writing this book. I delight in giving the credit where it belongs.

I want to thank my beloved wife, Rachel, who spent many lonely nights in bed as I stayed up late and wrote all that the Holy Spirit had placed in my heart.

To my beloved church, who has given me the opportunity to grow and experience so many different situations in life – thank you.

Thank you to Carmen Harrison, who has helped me with my grammar and spelling, and to Janet Angelo, my editor.

Foreword

Dear Reader,

It is my desire to teach you how to pray for your pastor. Many people think they know how to pray for their man or woman of God, but we do not need opinions. We need the direction of the Word of God. The prayers in this book are based on Psalm 45, a prayer of blessing for a king of Judah during a wedding. Even though a wedding prayer appears to be an unlikely place to begin the topic of intercession for pastors, it is actually one of the best places. I have come to this conclusion because this prayer of blessing includes the whole pastoral family. The kings of Israel and Judah were the shepherds of God's people, and we can draw direct parallels from the text to pray over our pastors.

I believe if you use these prayers as examples, guides, and outlines for praying for your pastor, then you will begin to see breakthroughs in the life of your congregation. God bless you, and may you not merely be a hearer of the Word, but a doer also.

Sincerely,

Cameron King

Table of Contents

Section 1

Praying for Your Pastor

Chapter 1

The Importance of the Pastor

*The LORD was with Jehoshaphat because
in his early years he walked in the ways
his father David had followed. He did not
consult the Baals but sought the God of his
father and followed his commands rather
than the practices of Israel. ⁵ The LORD
established the kingdom under his control;
and all Judah brought gifts to Jehoshaphat,
so that he had great wealth and honor.
His heart was devoted to the ways of the
LORD…*
(2 Chronicles 17:3-6)

*Jehoram received a letter from Elijah
the prophet, which said: "This is what
the LORD, the God of your father David,
says: 'You have not walked in the ways of
your father Jehoshaphat or of Asa king of*

*Judah... So now the LORD is about to strike
your people, your sons, your wives and
everything that is yours, with a heavy blow.*
(2 Chronicles 21:12 & 14)

Everything rises and falls on leadership.
John Maxwell

A No Good Terrible Bad Day

It happened to be just one of those mornings, which turned out to be one of those days. It started before we even left the bed. My wife rolled over, looked at the alarm clock, and shouted, "I have got to be at work in twenty-five minutes!" Even if she was dressed and ready, it's a twenty-five minute drive from our town to the next, and you guessed it, she works in the next town. Jumping to her feet she asked me to put some pop-tarts in the toaster. By the time they were ready, she was dressed and headed out the door. I made my way to the bedroom to dress. I got myself dressed, returned to the kitchen, and placed some toast in the toaster.

At that moment the phone started ringing. I picked it up and Rachel, my wife, was on the line. She informed me she was broken down on the side of Hwy 84. I would have shown a little more concern, but I noticed the toaster was on fire! The flames licking the bottom of my cabinets were about to singe them. My first thought was to unplug it, but that was ineffective. The flames still billowing out of my toaster were getting larger and larger. I picked up the toaster and tossed it out into the backyard. I had to hurry. My beautiful wife was stuck on the side of the road so I hopped in my car and sped to her rescue.

It was a smooth trip there and back, but when we arrived at home I discovered that my backyard was on fire, and my toaster was a black blob of melted plastic. I ran quickly and grabbed the garden hose to extinguish the fire. In the meantime, Rachel called her boss to tell him she was going to be late, and then she took my car and left for work.

After she departed, I suddenly realized that now I didn't have a ride to church. Furthermore, I remembered my abandoned vehicle on the side of the road and my lack of towing insurance. The matter was complicated additionally, because being a preacher, I found myself financially challenged. I had no desire to pay a wrecker to pick up my car. In light of the situation, I knew I needed Brother Jim. Jim is a retired manly-man who drives a dually, and even though he is much older than me, he seems like a much younger man. This is probably due to the fact that he works circles around ninety percent of men my age. I knew Jim could fix it. I called him, and he said, "I'll be there in about ten minutes, and I'll bring my chain." When I hung up the phone, I was pleased because I knew he would get the job done. Just like clockwork, Jim picked me up and we raced to my wife's car. He hooked the chain around the ball on his bumper and said, "I am going to pull you. You just need to keep the tension on the chain, and if you want to slow down just hit the brakes."

I said, "No problem."

I was a little nervous because I'm not very coordinated, and Jim was planning on towing my car on a highway with three too many red lights. We turned my vehicle around, and in no time flat we were traveling about seventy miles per hour. I was hitting the brakes in a fruitless attempt to tell Jim to slow down. The only problem was that his big old diesel truck never felt a tug when I hit the brakes. He was pulling me at seventy miles per hour. My brakes were smoking. He was running yellow lights, but by the time I made it through, they were red. I was praying as hard as I could. We finally made it to the mechanic shop, and he began to slow down and pull to a stop. He said, "What is that burning smell?"

I said, "That's my brakes."

He said, "That's funny, I never even felt you hit 'em." Then he said, "I thought from here we could push your car into the lot." I thought, *that's a great idea*. As we pushed the car through the parking lot, there was a pothole giving us trouble. We would push the car, hit the bump on the far side of the pothole, and then roll back.

I said, "Let's back up, then push the car forward quickly to get some momentum going." We did, and that car went right through that pothole. The only problem with this solution was the moment the car hit the pothole, it starting picking up more speed, and somehow, in just one second, we were trying to catch up with the runaway car. We finally caught the car, but only after it slammed into a truck. It did nothing to damage the truck, but it knocked out my headlight and put a huge scratch down the side of my car. I thought, *my troubles are never going to end,* but in reality they were just getting started.

We jumped in Jim's truck and he said, "You don't have a way to get around today, do you?"

"Nope."

Jim offered to let me borrow his truck for the rest of the day, and suggested he could pick it up that night at our church's Wednesday night gathering. I thought this was a great idea. I dropped Jim off at his house and returned quickly to mine. I thought, *you know, today has started off badly, so I'm going to start my day over. I'm not going to do anything stressful today.* I left my house to go to the Grady County Courthouse to take care of some personal business. As I arrived at the courthouse, I noticed all the parallel parking spots were empty. I said to myself, "Now I know my day is getting better." I had stood in line for about ten minutes when five city workers ran into the courthouse. This motley crew was shouting, "Who's driving the white dually?" These guys were taking down the city's Christmas lights, and I thought they needed me to move the truck so they could complete their task.

I shouted out, "That's me."

They shouted back. "A school bus was going down the road and it just slammed into the side of your truck, and the bad news is they never stopped."

Unbelievable. I went outside and sure enough the driver's side of the truck was deformed and maimed. A police officer stopped by and said, "This has not been your day has it?"

I said, "You don't know the half of it."

The police officer was logging all of the damage on the truck when the school bus returned to the scene. The lady driver shouted out the window, "I'll be back in just a little bit; I just have to finish my route."

The police officer shouted back, "You can't go anywhere! You're leaving the scene of an accident." Nonetheless, she drove away. The police officer said, "Follow me." I hopped into my wrecked, borrowed truck and began the police chase. The police car had its lights on and the siren blaring, and I was close behind.

He finally harassed the bus driver enough that she turned around and returned to the local high school. After the police officer gave her a first-rate chewing out, we assembled all of her insurance information and finally parted ways. The only reason I think he never arrested her is because she had a busload of special education kids. Now I was painfully aware of the fact that in a few hours I was going to have to tell Manly-man about his damaged truck. I arrived at church late that night because I knew Jim would be early. Forcing myself to walk into the building, I walked up to Jim and told him about the damage to his truck. He was not happy, but he took it in stride, as any godly man would do.

During that time we bussed in many street kids on Wednesday nights. Let's just say they were a little rough around the edges. I went outside to catch a breather and relax from my previous conversation. I was hoping I could minister effectively during the remainder of the night. The moment I walked out the door I saw our number one teenage troublemaker, Fred, punch a nine-year-old boy in the face on our basketball court. I ran up to him and shouted, "Get in the car! I am taking you home."

Fred said, "I am not going anywhere."

I calmly said, "Get in the car, Fred; I'm taking you home." Well about that time I thought Fred was going to turn around to get in the car, but in reality he was rearing back to punch me in the head.

The next thing I knew, my glasses were spinning around my head. I was thinking, *I can't believe it – this dope just punched me in the head!* The follow-through of his punch carried him away from me, and he fell to the ground. About that time he jolted to his feet and reared back again, and I thought, *He is getting ready to hit me again.* Before his second punch landed I tried to grab him, but he moved so quickly my armpit mashed into his face causing his neck to pop. He stood up straight and yelled, "My neck!" Then he collapsed right on the pavement. He looked like he was dead, and I just stood there staring at him, dumbfounded.

About that time many of the other kids started walking up shouting, "Hey, look, Pastor Cameron beat up Fred." I didn't care if Fred's neck was broken; I picked him up and placed him between two cars so no one could see the limp body lying at my feet.

As soon as I laid him on the ground, he popped up and screamed, "You just tried to kill me! I'm walking home and telling my parents what happened."

I calmly said, "Why don't you just stay here and let me get you some ice."

"I am going home," he spouted. He started walking home, and he did not allow me to give him a ride.

In light of the present development, I didn't care if it was church time; I was going to tell his parents what happened before he had a chance to give them his warped version of the story. I raced to his house, knocked on the door, walked in, and told his parents what happened. They appeared to believe me knowing the criminal history of their son. They assured me that everything was going to be all right, and said they were going to deal with his behavior. As I drove back to church I passed right by Fred, who was walking home. I asked Fred if he wanted a ride back home, and he did. Fred and I apologized and made up. I thought everything was cool. Nevertheless, when I got home that night, Fred's parents had called to ask my input in their decision to either sue me or press charges. They decided to call me repeatedly throughout the night to discuss the issue. I believe they thought a preacher beating up their kid would be a great opportunity to get some free cash. Too bad that wasn't the real story!

The next morning I met for prayer with some of my pastor friends, and we did spiritual warfare against the obvious attack of the enemy. Meeting with Fred's parents again, I convinced them it was in their best interest not to sue me. I reminded them I would hire my good friend, who is the best lawyer in town. I also let them know there was a yard full of witnesses that remembered the story like I did—

the way it really happened. Thankfully, they had a change of heart, and we mended the relationship.

If You Strike the Shepherd, the Sheep Will Scatter

My reason for telling this story is to illustrate the fact that the devil is actively attempting to oppose every single pastor in the world. This opposition comes in many forms and in many difficulties. The Bible is clear. If you "strike the shepherd, the sheep will scatter."[1] John Maxwell makes the statement that "everything rises and falls on leadership." This is certainly a true statement if you examine the scriptures. If you look at the scriptures I have listed previously, they show us that when the kings of Judah and Israel followed God, their nations prospered, but when the kings of Judah and Israel did evil, their nations were cursed.

The Hard Facts

The devil is fully aware that "everything rises and falls on leadership." Therefore, one of the devil's master plans, as he endeavors to keep churches in spiritual poverty, is to keep their leaders—their pastors—under constant attack. Only pastors can understand the violent spiritual battle that is constantly taking place around them. Many times pastors feel like Paul:

---

[1] Mark 14:27 & Zechariah 13:7

They are "hard pressed on every side."[2] Pastors often struggle with days and situations like the story I just shared. To the pastor, sometimes everything feels like an uphill battle. Don't think I am the only pastor who feels this way about the struggle of the ministry. Listen to these statistics given to us by Westwood Ministries...

- Eighty percent of pastors believe the ministry is affecting their family negatively.
- Seventy percent of pastors have no one they consider a close friend.
- Fifty percent of pastors have considered leaving the ministry in the last three months.
- Seventy percent of pastors say their self-esteem is lower now than when they began their ministry.
- Ninety percent of pastors say they are inadequately trained to cope with ministry.
- Fifty percent of pastors say they believe the ministry is hazardous to their health.
- One in five ministers today suffers burnout.
- One in three pastors finishes well.[3]

Maranatha Life does not have any good news about the state of our ministers, either. Look at these alarming statistics.

---

[2] 2 Corinthians 4:8

[3] Westwood ministries—www.westwoodministries.org

- Fifteen hundred pastors leave the ministry each month due to moral failure, spiritual burnout, or contention in their churches.
- Four thousand new churches begin each year, but over seven thousand churches close.
- Fifty percent of pastors' marriages will end in divorce.
- Eighty percent of pastors and eighty-four percent of their spouses feel unqualified and discouraged in their role as pastors.
- Fifty percent of pastors are so discouraged that they would leave the ministry if they could, but they have no other way of earning a living.
- Eighty-five percent of pastors said their greatest problem is they are sick and tired of dealing with difficult people such as disgruntled elders, deacons, worship leaders, worship teams, board members, and associate pastors. Ninety percent said the hardest thing about ministry is dealing with uncooperative people.
- Seventy percent of pastors feel grossly underpaid.
- Eighty percent of pastors' spouses feel their spouse is overworked.
- Eighty percent of pastors' wives feel left out and unappreciated by the church members.
- Eighty percent of pastor's spouses wish their spouse would choose another profession.

- Eighty percent of pastors' wives feel pressured to do things and be something in the church they really are not.
- The majority of pastors' wives surveyed said that the most destructive event that has occurred in their marriage and family was the day they entered the ministry.[4]

God Is Calling You to Help

These negative reports tell us the devil is seeking to destroy our pastors and their families. Someone needs to come to the aid of our pastors. The person God is calling to their aid is you. There are many things you can do to help your pastor, but the biggest is to pray for your pastor and his family. A spiritual problem requires a spiritual solution. The battle that rages around our pastors is intense, and they need some sheep that are focused on praying for their shepherd. I personally believe if our congregations around the world make praying for their pastors one of their top priorities, then the church around the world will begin to see revival and great awakening. Our pastors need us to pray for them, and this book is a guide for how we can bless our pastors in prayer.

---

[4] MaranathaLife.com

Chapter 2

What Do Wedding Songs and Pastors Have in Common?

For the director of music. To the tune of "Lilies." Of the Sons of Korah. A maskil. A wedding song.
(Introduction to Psalm 45)

Remember your leaders, who spoke the word of God to you. Consider the outcome of their way of life and imitate their faith.
Hebrews 13:7

No Teeth Make For Bad Wedding Days

While I was in El Salvador on my first mission trip, I was on a construction team helping to erect a new church in a small village. The team, in the middle of a project, was working hard. At that time, one of my fellow team members shouted, "Hey, catch" from the metal rafters above me. Looking up into the blinding Central American sun, I was frantically attempting to find the "thing" I was supposed to catch. I finally identified the three-foot level three inches before it plowed into my mouth. My first concern at the moment of impact was not the earthquake of pain that exploded in my head or the tsunami of blood that was cascading from my mouth. It was my teeth. The collision was so violent I could not feel anything below my nose but sporadic throbbing. Pulling upward on my upper lip, I turned to face one of my co-workers and asked, "Do I still have my teeth?" Much to my amazement he said, "Yes, but you are going to have to get stitches because your teeth went through your upper lip."

Many of the nationals suggested they walk me up to the village clinic. The kind missionary we were working with came running up to the helpful nationals who were walking with me, and he informed us I would not be going to the village clinic. I would be going to the national hospital. Thankfully I still had my teeth, but my concerns were not pain, blood, or stitches. My fear was rooted in my fiancé's reaction to this fiasco. I was getting married a week from the day my teeth were protruding out of my upper lip. I knew that if I spoiled our wedding pictures, I would be in more trouble than just getting stitches in a village clinic in a third world county!

In an overall sense, I was thankful for only a busted-up lip. Luckily, I have a mustache and a goatee that covered my stitches in an unnoticeable fashion. I was still a little apprehensive about introductions to new family members I had never encountered before. The apprehension grew at the thought of pictures immortalizing the second greatest day of my life (second only to salvation). My apprehension turned out to be needless; no one even noticed I had stitches. Even with a magnifying glass my stitches couldn't really be seen. By the grace of God, my wedding was saved and my scars were unnoticeable. This circumstance reminded me of one thing—No matter how macho a man is, he desires to look good on his wedding day. He wants to be at his best, and looking his best.

Why a Wedding Song?

Some people might wonder why I used Psalm 45 as a guide to help people pray for their pastor. When a person looks at the heading of Psalm 45, they read that it is a wedding song. This naturally begs the question, "What does a wedding song have to do with prayer, pastors, and anything having to do with church?" What you have to notice is who is getting married. It isn't just some casual marriage; this wedding ceremony is for royalty. It is for a king! The king of Judah or maybe Israel received this prayer of blessing on his wedding day. This prayer is for a person of influence. It is for a leader—a spiritual leader. Psalm 45 is a blessing spoken to a spiritual leader on his wedding day.

The Kings of Judah and Israel Were Their Shepherds

The Old Testament is clear: the kings of Israel and Judah were the nations' shepherds.[5] This suggests that the nature of pastoral ministry and the spiritual function of Israel's anointed kings were similar in character and function. The kings were the leaders of God's people on a national level. The pastors of our churches are the leaders of God's people on a congregational level. The kings of Israel and Judah were to protect the house of Jacob from spiritual danger, and the pastors of our congregations protect us from spiritual danger. The spiritual breakthroughs or the spiritual failures of the kings determined the direction of the whole nation either for good or for evil. In a similar fashion, the breakthroughs and failures of our pastors influence the whole of congregational life in a positive or negative manner.

A Scriptural Model

The psalmist goes through all of the blessings a spiritual leader needs to be successful. These blessings are necessary whether the leader is heading up a nation or a church. In light of this, Psalm 45 serves as a model of how to pray for our spiritual leaders.

If God in His wisdom gave us a model blessing to pray over our spiritual leaders, then we need to be faithful to implement that prayer in our lives. It

---

[5] 2 Samuel 5:2, 1 Chronicles 11:2, Ezekiel 37:24

should not matter if these spiritual leaders serve on a national, local, or congregational level.

The Royal Pastor

I am exceedingly glad Psalm 45 uses the vocabulary of royalty. Technically all true believers are royalty because we are the children of God—brothers and sisters with the King of kings and the Lord of lords. That places us within the royal family. When someone speaks of royal people, they are thinking of people of authority worthy of respect because of their position of power and leadership. They are people related to, or who have special relationships with, the king or queen. Is this not the nature of all of God's people, but especially the pastor? If we honestly examine our hearts, don't they testify that of all God's people, we owe our pastors the greatest respect? In terms of kingdom living, isn't it preeminent our pastors take up a royal disposition that affects their sphere of influence and their display of excellence? Is this not what the writer of Hebrews was communicating when he said the following, *"Remember your leaders, who spoke the word of God to you. Consider the outcome of their way of life and imitate their faith"*?

We owe our pastors respect. Yet, in my humble opinion (and based on my observation and experience), respect is one of the last things given to pastors in our society and in our churches. Whenever you talk to older pastors who have been in the ministry for a long time, many will inform you it is more difficult to pastor now than it was in times past. The reasons are rooted in many different things, but one major root is connected to a lack of esteem for spiritual leadership. I am not saying we are commanded to obey our pastors like kings, but what I am saying is we need to return to a place of showing honor, respect, and reverence for the men and women who watch over our souls.

It is my hope that this book will motivate you to intercede for your pastor, praying in faith that he or she will inherit the blessings of Psalm 45. I also anticipate, as you use the language of royalty found in this psalm, the Holy Spirit will place a greater respect in your heart for the man and woman of God in your life.

Chapter 3

The Noble Cause of Praying for Your Pastor

(Or, how the Holy Spirit stirs up concern for your pastor within your heart.)
My heart is stirred by a noble theme as I recite my verses for the king; my tongue is the pen of a skillful writer.
(Psalm 45:1)

A Shocking Debacle

One of my first experiences as a Spirit-filled believer was the collapse of the church where I had found Christ. Our church was attempting to refinance the mortgage on our building with a bond program. All of the bonds did not sell, and the church panicked because many members had placed their life savings in this mutually beneficial opportunity. When "hysteria" and "life savings" are coupled together in the same equation, it rarely ends with the phrase, "They lived happily every after." In this case, it led to a mass hemorrhage of people exiting our community of faith. (Their money was eventually returned to them.)

It was during this time that I observed the first pastor I ever considered to be "my pastor" struggling to keep it together. As the church began to slowly collapse around him, it appeared all the spiritual life he had within him began to ooze out under the pressure of imminent failure. It was not long after that he soon resigned. We found another willing soul to pastor our wounded congregation, but eventually the church closed.

Your Pastor Isn't Superman

During this time, it never occurred to me these pastors needed my prayers. I thought of them as the super-human type. They needed no prayer of mine; I needed theirs. Nevertheless, in spite of my glorified view of them, the burden of saving a sinking ship wore heavy on these men of God, who eventually could not hold up under such a heavy burden.

Since then I have become a pastor. I am also the president of the local ministerial association within our community. Every year I see pastors shuffle in and out of our community. Most come in with a blazing vision and a fire in their belly; most leave feeling like failures and with their head bowed in shame. I have become painfully aware that our pastors desperately need our prayers.

The Holy Spirit Gives the Desire to Pray for Your Pastor

Yet the psalmist wrote, "My heart is stirred by a noble theme." Whenever the people of God move in prayer for their spiritual leaders, especially their pastors, the Holy Spirit is stirring a noble theme in their hearts. The men and women of God who serve our congregations need Aarons and Hurs who hold the hands of their leader in the air during the intensity of battle.[6] When the fight is raging and our pastors become weak, the best way we can hold their hands in the air is by our prayers.

Many who read the book of Acts wonder why the power, passion, and sacrifice of the early church are absent in our present congregations. When was the last time your church called a prayer meeting just to pray for your pastor? When Peter was in prison, his congregation gathered specifically to pray for him. What happened when they prayed? An angel came to free him from prison. The trap the devil set for him was destroyed, and Peter was a free man.

The Key to Revival

What if the key to revival is praying for our pastors? What if the vast majority of Satan's traps intended to hinder and destroy our pastors were ruined because of an army of intercessors crying out for their pastors in prayer?

---

[6] Exodus 17:10-13

When we begin to bless our pastors through prayer, the Holy Spirit initiates a noble theme in our hearts. The compassion we sense for our pastors comes from God's Spirit. He skillfully guides us by His Spirit in prayer as we engage the Father for our pastor. When our pastors are strong, our churches are strong, and our communities get stronger. It is time for the people of God to rise up and say, "We will not allow another pastor to leave town in shame and disgrace." Imagine if we made our confession of faith, "No pastor is ever going to leave our church wondering what would have happened if they had been able to endure the battle. We will fight for them. We will pray for them. We will see them receive the victory. We will lift their arms in battle." It is the moment for us to give ourselves to this noble theme. It is time for us to pray for our pastors. It is time for us to make war for those who daily war on our behalf."

Chapter 4

The Excellent Pastor

You are the most excellent of men and your
lips have been anointed with grace, since
God has blessed you forever.
(Psalm 45:2)

The Shock of Culture and Religion

I am originally from the Greenville, South Carolina area, one of the biggest cities in the state. Greenville is a cosmopolitan city with its own unique urban atmosphere. Ironically, I moved from this metropolitan community to the most southern of South Georgia towns—Cairo. Arriving in Cairo at twenty-one years of age with youthful zeal and complete ignorance, I had an unquenchable desire to conquer the world. The first Sunday in the interview process at the church where I was a candidate brought out all eleven members, and when the vote was finally cast, two people decided to leave the church. Undaunted, I started with the remaining nine members, and by the second Sunday we had 15 people in attendance. I was ready to take on the town!

During that time there were no musicians in the church. I like to say we sang "karaoke style" to soundtracks and CDs. We worshipped to leaders like Darlene Zschech, Lendell Cooley, and Alvin Slaughter every week. We were blessed, but we were really motivated to transition to live music, and we believed God would bring the right people to our church to help us accomplish that. One Sunday night we had two visitors come by the church. They were both elderly women who appeared to have worshipful attitudes about them. For the sake of the story let's just call them Virginia and Bertha. After the service Bertha approached me and said, "I am going to help with your music." The commanding tone in her voice made me think, *I need to be careful with my words.* I said, "Sister, just keep coming to our church, and we'll see." That appeared to satisfy her, and I was just happy to have two visitors. We had grown to about twenty people, and I was ready to go to another level. The massive jump from twenty to twenty-two people is huge for a young pastor.

The next Sunday night rolled around and sure enough, there were Virginia and Bertha. Right on cue at the close of the service, Bertha approached me as though she were on a mission from God. When she got to the front of the church she said, "I am here to help you with your music."

I said, "Praise God!"

Then she said, "I am going to play the piano next Sunday night, and we ain't gonna do any of those new songs. This church is getting ready to do the sacred songs again."

I popped back, "I think we need to wait on that."

"What do you mean we need to wait on that?" she asked.

"Well ... a couple of things," I said. "First of all, you've never even made it to a Sunday morning service."

She said, "I play the piano at another church on Sunday morning so I won't be here on any Sunday morning."

I was starting to wonder if I could send this nut back to the peanut farm, but I was trying to maintain my composure. Then I said, "Well, I really don't think I want to lead the church in the direction of singing hymns."

After a ten-minute discourse on how hymns are from God and choruses are from the devil, her tirade finally ended. She was not at all fazed by the fact that I had no desire to do hymns. Finally I said, "Quite honestly, I don't know you. I have only met you one other time in my life, and I just want to get to know you before I put you on the platform as an example to others."

It was at that point that I thought her eyes were about to pop out of her head, and she shouted, "Get to know me?" Then she started to shout at the top of her lungs, "I know Dr. Addison." (Dr. Addison was the district leader of my denomination.) Every time, she shouted louder. "Get to know me? I know

Brother Addison." She probably shouted it about five times, but it felt like five thousand.

At this point, she had the attention of everyone in the church. When she noticed everyone in the building looking at her, she looked straight at them while pointing at me and shouted, "Crazy! That man is crazy!" Over and over again she shouted, "That man is crazy!" About that time Brother Howard began to laugh. Once he started laughing, one or two others began laughing. Within about 10 seconds almost everyone in the building was laughing, and it wasn't just the usual, polite kind of laughter you normally hear in church. They got hysterical in their laughter. It looked like a Rodney Howard-Brown revival on steroids.

About that time, Bertha hit a new level of anger when she discovered her charges of my insanity were falling on deaf ears and the seriousness of "her moment" had people bent over belly laughing. She continued on her rant, screaming, "You're all crazy! He's crazy, and you're all crazy. I am getting out of here." She stuffed her pocket book under her arm and burst through the door, which sent a second wave of hilarity rolling through the congregation, who had finally quieted down only moments before.

I looked over to her sister Virginia, who was still sitting there in the pew in shock. Virginia looked at me and said, "I am sorry she acts like that." That let me know this was common behavior for Bertha.

I said, "It's not your fault. Besides, you better hurry. It looks like she is going to leave you."

She said, "I am not going anywhere. If she wants me to ride with her then she will have to come back and get me."

Right when she said that, Bertha burst back into the sanctuary through the doors shouting, "Where's my sister?" In her mind we were holding Virginia captive. This resulted in a third wave of laughter. When Bertha saw that Virginia hadn't moved from her seat, she shouted angrily, "Come on!" Virginia meekly made her way to the door following meekly behind. The congregation was still trying to catch their breath from laughing so hard when the two sisters finally walked out of the church.

Bertha called me at the parsonage and let me have it one more time. Then she would call and hang up for about two hours. All the while, she was circling the city block where the church and parsonage sat.

She was so angry. To be honest, I was scared to death. I thought, *What if she has a gun? What if she breaks into my house and attacks, and I have to defend myself? That would look great in the city newspaper.* It would perhaps read like this, "Old lady in a rage attacks a pastor, and the pastor knocks her out!" *What if I have to call the police on this woman who appears to have lost her sanity?* She finally calmed down and went home. Bertha never came back to church, but Virginia became a great church member.

Excellence Is a Battle – Living It Is a War!

I tell you this story because it illustrates two things the writer of Psalm 45 asks us to pray on behalf of our spiritual leaders in verse 2. The writer yearns for our pastors to be people of excellence and to have their lips anointed with grace. The verse ends by telling us that God has blessed us, those of us in spiritual leadership, forever. He has blessed us with the ministry. Therefore we need to be men and women of excellence, and we need to be people who have their lips anointed with grace. This story shows us the enemy is fighting against the vision of pastors. If he can get pastors to compromise with another vision, this results in a failed vision, or at best a vision that is not carried out in a spirit of excellence. This story also illustrates how well meaning people with good intentions can stand in the way of excellence. Many people are oblivious to the fact that excellence is the goal of many pastors, and they certainly are unaware of the reality that their ideals could be preventing excellence from being obtained within the church. In this case, allowing a person to be on the worship team who was uncommitted to our congregation would *not* have set the precedent of excellence I was striving for in our church. Allowing someone to minister, who has an anger problem like hers, would have set a terrible example for our membership. I am still totally unaware if she possesses any talent. Talent and character are both variables in the equation of excellence. I absolutely know her vision for the church was not in line with mine or with that of the rest of our congregation.

In light of all this, well meaning but ignorant people are not the enemy. Many times these difficult people can be led toward excellence, but it is a process. The process takes great tact, grace, and wisdom with words. The process can only be completed by a person who has lips that are "anointed by grace."

Praying for Excellence

Pastors usually struggle with excellence in one of three ways, but before we look at these areas of struggle, let's look at the meaning of the word excellence. Excellence is translated from the Hebrew word *yapa*. This word means to be beautiful or delightful. It also means to adorn or make beautiful. Excellence is a concept that deals with every part of life from how we dress, to how we keep house, from how the church lawn looks, to how we prepare for a sermon. Excellence is doing things to the best of our ability for the glory of God. Excellence beautifies the world around us and makes it a better place. If the pastor's vision is going to be reached, then excellence must be a central priority within the process of taking steps toward fulfilling that vision.

Pastors' Three Struggles with Excellence

Pastors have three struggles with excellence. The first struggle deals with perfectionism. Excellence is doing our best for the glory of God. Perfectionism is excellence with a tendency toward legalism. Perfectionism does not measure us against our potential, but against perfection. Perfectionism is a tower of condemnation looming over pastors telling them that what they are doing will never be good enough. Many pastors struggle every day feeling their best will never be good enough, and that they are failures. Pastors need their people to pray that they will be free from the demon of perfectionism. When pastors are free of perfectionism, they can enjoy their progress and potential along the path of personal growth. The second problem pastors have with excellence is being oblivious to it. Every pastor has strengths and weaknesses. Some pastors have a propensity toward the ugly. They are totally okay with knee-high grass, unpainted buildings, trash that is waist deep in their car, and church toilets with trash bags draped over them because they have not been repaired in two years. Usually they are good pastors, but they are out of touch with the beauty of heaven and the reality that "Thy Kingdom come on earth as it is in heaven" includes beauty, quality, and a touch of elegance. Our pastors need our prayers to make them aware of the beauty of heaven. This awakening will result in excellence.

The final obstacle pastors have with excellence is maintaining it. Excellence requires money, time, and cooperation. It requires the gifts and talents of the entire congregation. If you remember the first part of the story, we were singing by CD at the beginning of my pastorate. There were no musicians in our church except Bertha. When I met Bertha, I was excited and thankful at first. The reason I was so excited was because I had became discouraged about our lack of musicians. I felt God deserved more than soundtracks. I was doing all I could do, but I was longing for a greater excellence in ministry. As you pray for your pastor, pray he will be connected to the people who will help him accomplish the measure of excellence he envisions in his heart.

Praying for Lips of Grace

Verse 2 also gives us another point to pray for our pastors. We are to pray that their lips are anointed with grace. It is one thing to speak the truth; it is another thing entirely to speak the truth in love. The harsh reality is pastors are surrounded by 'Berthas'. Yes, there are times when protection comes from belly-laughing congregants, but most of the time it does not. All pastors handle their 'Berthas' differently. Some pastors are intimidated and consequently give their 'Berthas' a fateful pass to the piano. Other ministers just avoid 'Bertha' altogether. When they see her, they walk the other way or make an emergency trip to the restroom. Then there is the pastor who allows 'Bertha' to make him angry. He speaks the truth, but he speaks it in anger. We cannot allow our natural tendencies to dictate how we deal with our 'Berthas.'

The effective pastoral confrontation is one of the most necessary but hated realities of serving in the ministry. Forceful Berthas must be told, "No," but they have to be told this in love. This requires lips that are "anointed with grace." Pastors have to deal with difficult issues all the time. We do not need to cower; we need to be bold. Yet we also need to speak the truth in a way that is not obnoxious, but clear and loving. That is a difficult combination, but that is why pastors need you praying for them. Pray their lips are anointed with grace.

Prayer for Our Pastors

Father, I come to You in the name of Jesus declaring that my pastor is a man of excellence. He is not bound or condemned by perfectionism, but he is able to see the beauty of Your coming kingdom and is well able to bring the excellence in his heart to the dominion around him. We thank You, Father, that You are bringing people with gifts, skills and talents to our pastor's side so he can have an expansion of excellence in his life, family, and ministry. Father, we also ask that his lips will be "anointed with grace." We thank You, Lord, that our pastor will never walk in intimidation; he will never avoid difficult situations or respond in anger to them. I ask that he will be able to speak the truth in love, and that everyone he speaks to will be captivated by the excellent combination of truth, love, and grace. In Jesus' name, Amen.

Chapter 5

The Prepared Pastor

*Gird your sword upon your side,
O mighty one; clothe yourself with
splendor and majesty.*
(Psalm 45:3)

Walking with Eyes Wide Open

In preparation for my first Easter at the church, many of the able-bodied members of our congregation gathered for a workday. It was the Saturday before Easter, and we were painting, cleaning, and working in the yards. It was a very tiresome day, but around 5:00 p.m. we finished. I was single at the time, so I didn't want to go back to my lonely parsonage. I decided I was going to prayer-walk the various neighborhoods surrounding the church. As I was walking and praying throughout the neighborhoods, I came close to our local diner. At that point,

I heard some strange rhythm and a mysterious beat. This was a unique phenomenon, because I hadn't noticed music in public since I had been in town. I started walking toward the music to see where it was coming from. I finally made it back to our church, but the sound was coming from the other side of the highway in a neighborhood I had never really explored. I thought there was no better time than the present, so I crossed the highway looking for this intriguing sound. As I walked a few blocks more, I began to recognize the sound of black gospel music. I thought to myself, *I love black gospel music; I have to find where this is coming from*. I finally came to a location where I knew the source was close, but still I could not locate it.

The Cat Was not the Only One Killed by Curiosity

I finally spotted a huge tent with music pouring out of it. I said to myself, *I am just going to peek into the tent and see what's happening*. I was not planning on staying because I still had on shorts and a T-shirt that were covered in paint, holes, sweat, and dirt. I was absolutely filthy. I pulled back the vinyl flap of the tent just enough to look in on the worship service. I was surprised to observe a packed house, and to my astonishment, I saw someone I knew standing on the platform. I had met this brother at the gym, and we had talked about the Lord a few times, but I never realized he was a church leader. His appearance shocked me a little, because he was wearing a gold metallic suit and tie with a bright red shirt. I said to myself, *I better get out of here before he sees me*, but I was too late. Right before I got my head out the tent flap he looked at me from the platform and said, "Reverend King, come on in and join us." I was waving and mouthing "no." Yet, before my response registered, he told everyone to, "Stand up, and give Reverend King a round of applause as he makes his way to the platform." I stepped completely into the tent so he could see my attire. I was waving, mouthing, and begging *no!* Nevertheless, everyone on the platform stood up and started shouting and waving me down the aisle. "Come on, Reverend King," they shouted. So I made my way down the aisle in my shorts and T-shirt covered in paint and sweat while everyone in that tent was cheering and shouting for me. I finally made it onto the platform while my friend in his metallic suit informed the crowd that, "after Pastor Jones speaks, Reverend King will be sharing the Word." Upon hearing that bit of information, my jaw almost hit the ground. Then he went on to say, "But now let's finish praising the Lord."

At that point, we went into a heavenly time of worship. I nearly forgot I was in the order of service. When the music began to die down, a lady named Evangelist Smith got up, grabbed the microphone, and shouted at the top of her lungs, "God's going to kill you." Needless to say, she had my attention.

She launched into her evangelist appeal at the top of her lungs: "I know all of you people in these houses around here can hear me. That is why we have this sound system turned up so loud. Cause I know, you're like Nicodemus. You're afraid to come out in the dark. And I have a word for ya. God is going to kill you! I was preaching in New York City right in the projects, and this same word came to me that God is going to kill you, and people started dying in those projects. There were notices every day in that apartment that someone had died. So repent of being like Nicodemus. Get out of your house and get in here. I know you can hear me. This whole neighborhood can hear me. So come on out."

I thought to myself, *I don't think that would make me want to come out.* Then my mind began to wander as I thought of the ten million ways this address to the neighbors could have been handled differently. The time finally arrived for Pastor Johnson to speak, and I was happy because it was getting late, and I wanted to be ready and rested for my first Easter message the next morning. Pastor Johnson announced in a high-pitched yet gruff voice that he was planning to preach on the Ten Commandments. Much to my surprise Pastor Johnson did two unexpected things (at least, from my perspective). First, he preached on the first two commandments for two hours. Secondly, he made me his source of authority forcing me to back up everything he said. This would have been all right had I agreed with his applications or his rabbit trails within the message. I began to feel uncomfortable when he said, "All these preachers are preaching from all these other Bibles, these NIV Bibles, these New American Standard Bibles, these Living Bibles, but there ain't but one Word of God, and that is the King James Bible. It-n-that right Brother King?" My eyes were as wide as saucers. However, that wasn't the end of his pleas for confirmation during his message. It went on call after call, and it went like this…

"I walked into the church one day, and there was a picture of Jesus hanging on that wall, and I told them to tear it down. 'Thou shall not make any graven images of the Lord thy God'. It-n-that right Brother King? All these preachers studying for their sermons, writing out all their notes. God said, 'I will give you the words in that hour.' Ain't that right Brother King? We're out here trying to win souls, and we can't get no preachers out here to help us. It-n-that-right Brother King?" Every time, I just sat there like I was lost in the spirit. I had my legs crossed, my hands on my knees, and my eyes squinted closed. I was humming with my mouth shut, nodding my head back and forth as if in agreement, the whole time.

Hypocrisy Needed

Was that hypocrisy? Absolutely! There are times for acting and there are times for being genuine. Nevertheless, when you are covered in dirt and paint while everyone else is dressed to the max, that is not the time to be the voice of controversy. That is the time to blend in. Who am I to say anything different? I do use the NIV Bible, and I practically preach from a manuscript! Who am I to say that perhaps the best way to get other pastors involved is to communicate with them that you are having an event?

Skipping Out Early

When he was about two hours into the sermon and still had eight commandments to go, I leaned over to a man I had never met, but I'd heard him introduced as "Deacon," and so I said, "Deacon, I'm getting ready to leave."

Deacon said, "You can't leave now, you have to preach after he finishes."

I said, "Deacon, I don't think they are going to miss me. Besides, he has eight commandments to go."

Deacon whispered to me, "I am sure he will finish up in thirty minutes."

I said, "It is almost eleven o'clock. I'm just going to slip out the back curtain. You guys can make it without me." At that point, I stepped out of the opening in the tent and quickly started walking home.

Deacon started running after me shouting, "Reverend King, you are up to preach next." I turned and shouted, "I think you can make it without me." Then I turned and ran as if I were running for my life.

Looking back on this experience, I can summarize it by saying I was totally unprepared. I was unprepared in my attire. I was unprepared to preach. I was unprepared to handle conflict. I was unprepared for the entire situation I had walked into.

Ready for Battle

Verse 3 tells the spiritual leader to "gird your sword upon your side, O mighty one." This refers to being prepared for battle. Every minister of the gospel needs to be prepared. Paul tells us to be prepared in season and out of season.[7] It could be due to the nature of my personality, but I have walked into so many experiences I was not prepared for. The story above is one of many examples. I have talked to plenty of ministers who have had an overabundance of situations and difficulties they were not prepared to meet. Many of these ministers resigned from their post prematurely due to being unprepared and over-whelmed. Conflicts, spiritual battles, slander, people leaving, and people's sins are all common things pastors have to deal with. No matter how much they pray and study, sometimes pastors will be hit with situations that leave them feeling ill equipped. The constant battle pastors face takes the greatest toll on their spiritual strength in the ministry. When these hard-hitting battles begin to rage, it is usually during a time when they are not prepared. The process of readjusting to an unexpected battle usually zaps a pastor's spiritual strength in an especially potent fashion. This is why pastors need people praying for them. Pastors need intercessors pleading on their behalf that they will be prepared for unforeseen battles in the ministry. They need people who will

---

[7] 2 Timothy 4.2

cry out to God that a sword will be girded to their pastor's side.

Our pastors need to be prepared. They need to spiritually prepare for the battle by awakening themselves to the Lord's presence through prayer, the Word, and by actively using their spiritual gifts. They need to mentally prepare through a constant diet of training, learning, and equipping. The personal and professional development of the minister is imperative if he is going to stay healthy, strong, and ready for the battle. The final ingredient is for us to pray that our pastors will activate all that is within them so they can lead us to the place of victory.

Clothed in Honor

Verse 3 also tells the pastor to "clothe yourself with splendor and majesty." Splendor and majesty are terms that speak of royalty. People in royal families have confidence, glory, and honor. Pastors are royal people in a royal family; therefore they should be clothed in confidence, and they should carry themselves with honor.[8] When I experienced the previous story, I certainly was not clothed in splendor, majesty, honor, or confidence. I looked like a vagabond. I am not saying a pastor should wear a suit all the time. What I am saying is they need confidence. They need to carry themselves in a manner that conveys their confidence in knowing they are victorious. You need to pray that your pastor will remain calm and

---

[8] I Peter 2:9

confident and that he will lead the church into greater spiritual maturity.

Prayer for Our Pastors

Father, we come to You in the name of Jesus. Right now we ask You that our pastor will be ready for every battle he faces. That no matter what difficulty he is dealing with in the church or in his personal life, he will be prepared. Remind him that the Word of God on his side has equipped him for that very moment, and reassure him that in the battle he will be filled with faith and confidence. We also pray that our pastor will be confident in everything he puts his hand to, and that this confidence will lead to victory in every battle and will remove discouragement from his life. In Jesus' name we pray, Amen!

Chapter 6

The Victorious Pastor

In your majesty ride forth victoriously in
behalf of truth, humility and righteousness;
let your right hand display awesome deeds.
Let your sharp arrows pierce the hearts
of the king's enemies; let the nations fall
beneath your feet.
(Psalm 45:4-5)

An Opportunity to Serve

Even though I was in my first pastorate and we were a small church, I felt we could do great things for God. An area I saw as one of the greatest needs in our community was poverty. Poverty is a huge issue, but we saw that we could make a difference, especially with teenagers who were living in poverty. We started picking up teenagers who lived in nearby neighborhoods. Most of these teens came from broken homes that were being destroyed by drugs, alcohol, sexual abuse, and perversion in the lives of their parents. Many of these kids were failing in school. Sexual promiscuity was rampant, and several of these kids were already experimenting with drugs. Many of these children had never been disciplined or trained how to act properly as citizens, much less as Christians. The church and I were trying to make a difference. Needless to say, attempting to influence these kids for the gospel was difficult, and it was a huge uphill battle.

Going Nowhere

One of my lowest points in the battle for these kids was on a Saturday driving back from Atlanta. We were returning from a denominational youth event. I was a little discouraged because it appeared that God touched all the kids at the event except for the teens I had brought. As I was fighting off discouragement, the bus began to gargle, and the next thing we knew we were stranded on the side of I-75 in the middle of nowhere. Our cell phones were dead; the sheriff's office would not help us because they thought transporting so many children would be a liability. Finally, some strangers stopped by who were willing to transport the thirty teenagers and the chaperones to the nearest truck stop. There we waited three hours for several church members to make their way to our location to pick our crew up.

All in all, we were stranded on the side of I-75 for about three hours and then sat at the truck stop for three more hours. It was a constant struggle to keep these kids in order. As I reflected on the disaster during the long ride home, I knew I was in the center of God's will, but I also understood I was not being effective at accomplishing God's will. I rediscovered God's heart for these unchurched teens of all races and backgrounds, but I also wondered if I was making a difference. There were no signs these teens were experiencing a change of heart in any way. Doing the will of God with no visible signs of success can be discouraging beyond my ability to communicate.

You Never Feel Weak When You Are Strong

I also remember a time when our church was steadily growing. Parking was a concern, space in the sanctuary was an issue, and finding enough room for all our ministries was a challenge. Yet, these were great issues to have. We were growing and we needed to build. We launched a building program that was a huge success. We were able to relocate from our old traditional and landlocked sanctuary to a brand new facility on fifteen acres of land. We were miraculously able to purchase the largest undivided piece of property in the city limits. The people were giving, and we were able to build a million dollar facility with limited debt. All of this took place in one of the poorest regions in the United States. Conversions were a common occurrence, our ministries were growing, and there were accomplishments at every turn. I never grew tired, because there was success in everything we did.

The writer of this passage of scripture in the book of Psalms prays victory for his spiritual leader. "In your majesty ride forth victoriously in behalf of truth, humility and righteousness; let your right hand display awesome deeds." The heart of greatness is in the chest of almost every pastor I have ever met. All pastors desire to accomplish the will of God, yet many feel trapped. These pastors are attempting to accomplish the will of God with no sign of God moving and with no indicator of success in sight. This is how I felt after the bus breakdown on the side of I-75 with thirty unruly teenagers. I knew the will of God. I could see God's heart on the matter, but I was powerless to accomplish it. There is no feeling more desperate or depressing.

Victory is in the heart of every pastor. When our church growth was exploding right before our building program, nothing was greater. The joy of accomplishing the vision God placed in my heart was unparalleled to any other joy in life. Yes, some joys are greater, but this joy is unique. The satisfaction of victory is incredible. Nevertheless, most pastors do not feel this sense of victory, accomplishment, and success often enough, if ever at all. Our job is to ensure our pastors have the prayer support that is going to lead them into victory.

The Foundation of Victory

The foundation of victory is the same as the purpose of victory. For the kingdom of God to advance, it must have leaders who are rooted in truth, humility, and righteousness. There is a need for pastors who are men and women of God to be honest in their transactions, their words, and in their messages. Leaders who are humble enough to see their dependence on God, meek enough to keep learning and growing, modest enough to see their mistakes and learn from them, are the ministers that will be victorious. Pastors are to be men of holiness who walk in the biblical standard and possess integrity that cannot be shaken. It is only when pastors begin to walk in these virtues that they can be trusted with success and victory.

The Purpose of Victory

In a very general sense the purpose of any victory in ministry is to advance these virtues. God has established that the means of ministry shall not violate the goal of ministry. God is so adamant about this reality that the only way true success in the ministry can be achieved by His people is that they function in these virtues. No matter how grand the result, it is only accredited to our heavenly account when our labor is carried out in His ways—truth, humility, and righteousness. The uncommon and unusual reality of ministry is found in this biblical principle. The principle is that the *foundation* of victory is the same as the *outcome* of victory. God does not want evangelism that does not spread truth, humility, and righteousness. The Father desires church services conducted in truth, humility, and holiness. The Father still longs to be worshiped in Spirit and truth. God is still searching for worship that cries out to Him in humble dependence and desperation. The Father is seeking a heart of passion that lifts holy hands to the throne of God. There is no fellowship within the family of God without these realities. Any endeavor to disciple new believers or any other function conducted within the church without these three virtues will result in a lack of credibility that will rob the church of its fruit. Any act of service, evangelism, worship, discipleship or fellowship that is void of these three virtues may at times give the appearance of victory from an earthly perspective, but from heaven's viewpoint they are only a miserable disappointment that fails to give God the glory He deserves, while at the same time grossly misrepresenting the nature and character of the God we wish to glorify. That is why the writer prays that his spiritual leader will "ride forth victoriously in behalf of truth, humility and righteousness." Our prayer should be the same for our pastor. Our pastors need the foundation of victory—truth, humility, and righteousness. They also want the fruit of victory—more truth, humility, and righteousness.

Awesome Deeds and the Glory of God

The psalmist also cries out to God that his leader's right hand will "display awesome deeds." The psalmist's desire is not solely the king's effectiveness at accomplishing the will of God, but that in the accomplishment of God's will, the glory of a greater kingdom will be displayed. The king's victories should always lead to God's glory. This glory comes when the fruit produced by the pastor's hands is greater than his own ability, talent, or skill; the fruit is so great that only the hand of God could have accomplished it. Thus, the greater kingdom will have emerged within our pastor's domain.

Our prayers concerning our pastors should ask the Father to help them accomplish the will of God. At the same time, however, they are to accomplish His will in such a way that proves God Himself accomplished these things through them. Supernatural effectiveness is possible. This can be observed throughout all of Scripture. Our prayer should be, "Lord, do awesome deeds through our leaders; give them the supernatural power to accomplish the vision You've placed in their heart in such a way that You receive the glory."

The writer then gives us the other key to victory that our prayer can unlock for our pastor. He goes on to say, "Let your sharp arrows pierce the hearts of the king's enemies; let the nations fall beneath your feet." As I mentioned earlier, most pastors experience spiritual warfare on a fiercer level and on a more consistent basis than most people ever encounter personally. It is not in God's plan that our pastors have to face this battle alone. You are to cover them in prayer, believing that every demon of hell that attacks your pastor will be struck down with the angelic arrows of heaven; that every people group your pastor longs to reach with the gospel will be reached; and that every demonic force that has blinded these people will fall at his feet.

God has given your pastor a vision to reach your community, and your prayers should help him to accomplish all that is in his heart. You are to bombard heaven crying out for the victorious charge of your pastor that every enemy of hell standing in his way will fall at his feet.

Prayer for Our Pastors

Father God, I come in the name of Jesus on behalf of my pastor. I pray that he will be a man that is rooted and established in truth. No deception will cover his eyes, and truth will be his primary mode of operation. I also ask that he will be a man of humility, never forgetting that he is dependent upon You, and that his humility will motivate him to learn, grow, and listen to the counsel of others. I also pray that he will be a man of righteousness who understands his right place in You, and that condemnation will not attack him. Integrity will be the only manner in which he acts, and holiness will be the passion of his heart. Lord, as he walks in these truths, I pray he will ride forth in victory spreading truth, humility, and holiness. I believe what You have placed in his heart will be accomplished by his hand, resulting in an understanding by all people that these accomplishments were conducted by the power of God rather than the strength of man. I ask, Lord, the result

*of all his victories will be the glory of God;
I also stand against every enemy that would
attack my pastor. Let every demonic force
be destroyed and removed from his path,
and let every person who opposes him in the
natural realm repent and be free from the
influence of the evil one. I thank you, Lord,
that every people-group Pastor desires to
reach will be reached because the nations
are falling at his feet. In Jesus' name, Amen.*

Chapter 7

The Lasting Pastor

*Your throne, O God, will last forever
and ever; a scepter of justice will be the
scepter of your kingdom.*
(Psalm 45:6)

L et me tell you a few random stories that have
nothing to do with each other, but that have a
common theme woven among them all.

Freezing Cold in the Will of God

The day I arrived in Cairo, Georgia, to live was
a warm winter day in January. Even though the
calendar said it was winter, it felt like spring. As I
was moving into the parsonage, many of the church
members asked if I wanted to fix the heat. Because
it was warm that day I just said, "All I care about
is the air conditioning." They said, "That's really all

you need here, anyway." Winter came and winter left, and what the native Georgians said proved to be true. I did not know that it was unseasonably warm that year. Spring, summer, and fall all came and left with no need of heat. We were in the middle of the following winter and there was still no need for heat until one cold morning. On this morning I awoke around 6:30 in the morning, and I thought frost was on my face and bed. It was about ten degrees below freezing outside, and I had no heat in the house! The house was not winterized, and it felt like the jet stream was flowing under my sheets.

I called Layla Smith, the church treasurer, and asked her to call an electric company to come out and get a heater installed in my old, historic house. She called around for me and told me that heaters were backordered for weeks in the city, county, and surrounding counties. Because I lived in a very old house, with very old gas piping, I could not just run to the nearest Lowe's and get a heater. She also informed me that because of my aggressive history in repairing the church, we would need a couple more offerings to pay for the heater anyway. This was no comfort to me.

At that point I called my dad, an official junk man, and asked him if he had a heater that could be installed. He had one, but he could not make it until the weekend, and it was Monday. Oh, did I mention that my office was in the freezing, cold house as well? Needless to say that was a long, cold week, but by Saturday dear old Dad had bailed me out.

Crazy Times

This second story took place some time later. Our church has always tried to reach the people in our community that other churches are not reaching. As providence would have it, most of these people were extremely poor. It also seems that a high percentage of these people suffer from some form of mental illness. One of them was Lucy, and Lucy was not mentally ill. Lucy was crazy. She kept everything she owned in her Chevy S-10 truck. If the government agencies (whom she was certain were seeking her) came looking for her, she could leave immediately. She also wore hats so the FBI would not be able to locate her. Of course, she informed us that she was on the FBI's most wanted list. Lucy never thought that there was anything strange about her behavior, but she claimed to have Tourette's Syndrome because she cursed. I never believed that she actually had Tourette's Syndrome, because she never cursed until something made her angry.

It was a warm Sunday night when Lucy saw some of our teenagers partaking in behavior that was inappropriate, so she took it upon herself to give our youth a "good cussing-out." About that time, a few adults ran into the building to tell me that Lucy was "cussing our kids out" in the parking lot. I ran out very quickly because most of our kids received verbal abuse at home, and I was going to make sure it never took place at church. I told Lucy to stop cursing at our kids, and if they did something bad, she could come get me to deal with it. This process was repeated two more times during the night. Then Rachel, my new wife, said, "Let me go and talk to her." When Rachel went outside to talk to her, Lucy grabbed Rachel by the lapels of her shirt, pulled her up to her face, and cursed her for everything she was worth. Rachel wrestled away from her and came running inside— disheveled. When I heard what had happened, I ran outside to make sure she was going to leave the property. I found Lucy alone screaming every four letter profane word in the English language. I told her that if she did not leave I was going to call the police and have her arrested, and then I was going to call the FBI to inform them she was captured. When that thought hit her, she got in her loaded truck and headed home.

I thought the battle was over, but then she began calling all the board members in the church telling them I needed to be fired. This did not bother me until one day when she called Layla Smith, the church treasurer, and told her the story from her perspective. Then Layla said, "Lucy, you're acting like he hit you." There was a sudden pause, and then Lucy said, "He did hit me." This was never in the story until that moment. Lucy still believes I hit her that night. At point, she began to call every person in the church to tell them that I beat her up in the church parking lot. That effort came to no avail, so she called every other minister she knew in town and started telling them "the story." Then for two weeks her family kept threatening to sue me for the imagined act of violence. That was not a fun two weeks.

A Mass Exodus

The final story took place in the new church. I was preaching one Sunday on racial reconciliation. I really did not think this was a touchy subject because our church was already multicultural, and I thought that if a person did not like being with people of other races, then they would never come to our church. At the same time I thought everyone could get a little better at being a cross-cultural missionary. I preached on Acts 15 and gave some key points that would help us with cross-cultural ministry. After that service, thirty people decided to leave the church. Many of these people were strong leaders, strong givers, and strong influencers. They never returned.

The Enemy Brings Discouraging Circumstances

The common theme running through all of these stories is that I wanted to quit after each crazy occurrence happened. One of the major schemes of the enemy is to cause circumstances that will bring discouragement and depression to pastors. The devil knows that if he can "strike the shepherd, then the sheep will scatter.[9]"

The thrust of this verse deals with legacy, and the greater legacy usually corresponds with greater longevity. The psalmist's prayer goes like this, "Your throne, O God, will last forever and ever." We know

---

[9] Mark 14:37 & Zechariah 13:7

this prayer was offered for a king from Judah, because these kings were given the Davidic promise that his throne would endure forever[10]. This prayer was more than likely offered for Solomon or Hezekiah, but it was pointing to an even greater king whose throne will last forever. It pointed to King Jesus, who will rule over the Messianic Kingdom. His throne and His rule will have no end.

Now bringing this back to the topic of praying for our pastors, I am in no way suggesting that a pastor is a king that rules from the throne within the church. I certainly am not suggesting that a pastor's rule is forever. These things would be unbiblical.[11] Actually, all believers are kings and priests of God,[12] and we hold that position for all of eternity. We know a pastor's tenure is not eternal, yet his influence can be. This issue can be paradoxical, because the eternal impact of a pastor usually increases exponentially with the longevity of his or her tenure. Therefore, one of the strategies of the kingdom of darkness is to keep a continual bombardment of problems flowing in the pastor's direction. The purpose and plan behind these problems is to bring the pastor to a place where he is ready to relocate, move on, or quit.

---

[10] 2 Samuel 7:11

[11] Acts 15:28—The early church used consensus as the primary means of making decisions. None of the "spiritual giants" of the Bible appealed to who they were as a basis for making decisions.

[12] Revelation 1:6 & 5:10

Praying for Legacy

Our prayer for our pastor should be that his influence "will last forever" and his impact will be eternal. Keeping these realities in mind and understanding they are going to increase with the longevity of his tenure, we need to protect our pastor from the constant onslaught of attacks that manifest themselves in a never-ending occurrence of problems. These problems drain a pastor spiritually, discourage him emotionally, weaken him physically, steal time from his family, and keep his eyes off the call God has placed on his life. When a pastor has to relentlessly deal with a parade of problems at a particular church, the likelihood of his remaining at that church for the long term is improbable. If his eternal godly influence and impact is to be on our life and the lives of our children and grandchildren, and he does not achieve the eternal impact that Christ intends, then the only person who is really losing out is us. Let's keep our pastor in our prayers, believing that he will be protected from problems that might result in his premature resignation from the congregation—and thus stealing from his eternal impact on our congregation.

The Straight but Difficult Path

The second portion of the verse tells us that "a scepter of justice will be the scepter of your kingdom." The kingdom of God is a kingdom of justice. If the kingdom of God is going to advance through our churches, then it has to start with the pastor. If the pastor is going to have influence forever as well as an eternal impact, then he or she must lead with justice. The Hebrew word for justice is *misor.* [13] This word means plateau, plain, level ground, of right ruling and living, and uprightness. Serving justice means bringing people to level ground. It is living and leading based on God's principles. The application of this phrase could entail a whole book in and of itself; however, let's take these next few thoughts with us. The pastor's decisions need to be based on what is true and what is right. It is easy to overlook the sin of a leader who is talented or wealthy. It is unproblematic to always side with the people in the church you have a tendency to enjoy naturally rather than the ones who get on your nerves. It is simple to allow the poorer members of your congregation to receive second-class pastoral care. Yet, the pastor is to be a man of principle, and these principles are to be rooted in justice. When this occurs, the pastor will gradually gain greater respect. There may be times when the people in the church do not agree with the pastor's decision, but if he has a history of leading with justice, then the congregation will be settled in the fact that his reasoning is rooted in the truth of Scripture. This will make it easier for them to follow or confirm the decisions of the pastor.

---

[13] Strongs # 4793

Prayer for Our Pastor

*Father, I come to You in the name of Jesus,
and I pray that my pastor will have an
eternal impact and that his influence in this
church will be felt positively for generations to come. I also pray that he will stay
in this church as long as Your will permits.
While he leads our church, I pray he will
be protected from senseless problems that
would drain him spiritually and discourage
him emotionally. When he does leave, I
pray it will be at Your leading and not due
to a lack of care from our congregation. I
pray he will be blessed spiritually, emotionally, and physically. I pray he will have
time with his family and that his finances
will be blessed. I believe that our pastor
will have an awareness that he is making a
difference for the kingdom of God and that
his influence will expand internally within
the church, outwardly within the community, and eternally within generations to
come. I pray his impact will be powerful,
fruitful, and effective, and that nothing will
discourage him to the point of giving up.
Father, I also ask that he will lead in justice.
Let his leadership decisions be based on the
truth of Scripture and not the pressures of
the moment. I ask that our pastor will make*

decisions that are right, true, and according to Your will. In Jesus' name, Amen!

Chapter 8

The Anointed Pastor

*You love righteousness and hate wick-
edness; therefore God, your God, has
set you above your companions by
anointing you with the oil of joy.*
(Psalm 45:7)

A Miraculous Summer

When I was attending Southeastern University in Lakeland, Florida I was praying after class one day in the prayer chapel. While I was praying, I felt the Lord speak to my heart. He said, "I want you to preach revivals this summer while you are home from school."

I replied to God, "But, Lord, I don't know any pastors, and if you are going to preach revivals, then you have to know pastors."

The Lord spoke back to me, saying, "I will whisper your name in the wind, and pastors will hear it." It was at the end of the semester and I would soon head home for the summer. I knew God would have to confirm what I thought He said. I also understood confirmation would result in some form of preaching date. I knew I could not preach at my home church, because I didn't have much experience preaching, and our church attendance ran over a thousand on Sunday mornings. In light of this, I called my Granny and asked if she would talk to her pastor about me to see if he would allow me to preach at her small holiness church. I thought if there was a church that was going to allow me to speak with as little preaching experience as I had, it would be Granny's church. The hunch turned out to be true. Not only did I get to preach Sunday morning and night, they asked me to preach a mini revival that ran through Wednesday night.

Things were off to a great start, but I was surprised at how well things turned out. The Holy Spirit moved powerfully during that revival, and it rolled on for two weeks. During that two-week period, several pastors and associate pastors visited the church. During the course of the two-week revival, I was able to fill my calendar for the summer with preaching dates. I held revivals until I returned to school. God is faithful!

I recognized that God had called me to a task, and the task was accomplished. During that time God anointed me to accomplish His will for the summer. This brought joy to my heart. The anointing is God's power to do God's work. This anointing did not just appear. The cultivation of this anointing started as I began to value scriptural holiness. Almost a year earlier, my youth pastor had preached a message on holy living and I felt deep conviction. I made immediate and dramatic changes in my life, and from that point until now, the anointing has been growing. Sometimes the power is stronger than at other times, but the ebb and flow of the anointing usually increases as I walk in greater surrender to God.

Conducting ministry without the anointing can only be likened to hell on earth. Therefore, it is our job to pray that our pastors will have the anointing. The anointing will bring them joy. It is one thing to preach a series of revivals and then return to your home church. It is totally different to pastor a church full-time. Pastoring is difficult, and it places a constant demand on the power of God that is at work within the pastor. Pastors need the anointing. They need it in an overabundant amount.

The Anointing Brings Joy

This verse tells us when a pastor hates what is evil and loves what is holy, there is a blessing that comes with that disposition. That blessing is the anointing. The anointing is God's power to do God's work. The anointing brings joy to your life because the anointing makes you effective. Effectiveness brings you opportunity. Opportunity will bring you exaltation. All of the above will bring joy to your heart[14].

---

[14] I know that many people think we pastors should be so spiritual that we don't need any recognition. Yet no one is really

Unexpected Exaltation

When I was a senior in high school, I was praying that God would open an opportunity for me to do ministry. My mother, on the other hand, was praying I would get a job and make money because I was headed off to college. God was more than able to answer both prayers. A few months earlier, a few of us in the youth group decided to go to Applebee's to get some riblets after drama practice one night. While we were waiting to be seated, we ran into the minister of music from one of the larger Baptist churches in our area. We did not think anything about it, and we were seated. We ate our rib feast with joy. Tex, the minister of music, jotted my name down in his notebook, and we both forgot about the meeting.

A few months later, after my mother came home from work one day, she received a call from Tex. Tex explained that he had been looking for someone to fill a temporary staff position to help with their summer programs and also to organize an Olympic rally in our community. Our community was not far from Atlanta where the 1996 Olympic Games were being hosted. He explained they had been looking to fill the position for about six months. They had called all of the seminaries in the southeast region to spread the word, but they had received no response. They had called every campus ministry at every state

---

that spiritual. The Bible says that when we humble ourselves, then God will lift us up. It is not wrong to be lifted up, and it is certainly not unsatisfying to be lifted up. Our job is to allow God to lift us up, and not to endeavor to lift ourselves up.

college in the state, but no one was interested. There was a Baptist college in our community, but no one from that school was interested either.

The only thing that had come to Tex's mind was that boy he'd met at Applebee's about four or five months earlier. Tex had found the notebook he'd written my name in and called my mother to see if I was willing to work for them during the summer. When he told her how much money I would make, she just about shouted! My mother asked, "When would you like him to start?"

He said, "Tomorrow! But first, I need to talk to him and then get him approved with the pastor. When he gets home from school, can he meet us at the church?"

Mother said, "Sure!" When I arrived home that day, Mother said, "The Lord has answered our prayers. You can do ministry, and you will get paid too."

Later, when I walked into Tex's office, I saw that two other staff members were there to assist with the interview. They all gave their approval, and they took me to meet me the pastor. Tex walked into the pastor's office and said, "We want to hire Cameron King to fill the summer staff position."

The pastor said, "Cameron King ... that's the fanatic at the high school, right?"

Tex said, "Yes, I think so."

Pastor said, "Let's hire him; we need some fanatics around here."

Tex said, "The only problem is that Cameron still has two and a half weeks of school left, and we need him to start tomorrow." Pastor called me in and said, "You are a senior right?"

I said, "Yes."

Then he said, "How are your grades?"

I said, "Great. I expect to make all A's this year." My high school allowed seniors who had earned all A's during the entire duration of the year to exempt their final exams. Final exams made up the last week of school, and seniors just studied and reviewed for final exams the week before. With this knowledge in mind, Pastor stated, "So then you really don't need to be at school for the last two weeks. What is just a few more days of missing school? I know the principal; you don't have to worry about going back to school this year. You will get out two and half weeks early." He called the principal immediately, and when he got off the phone he said, "Be here at work tomorrow."

It turned out to be an experience of a lifetime. It was the first time I had been involved in a mega-church. (I was attending a smaller church at the time. My family had not yet switched to the larger church that I mentioned earlier.) I was allowed to sit through staff and board meetings. They paid for me to go on a mission trip to the state of New York and work with Muslim children. I helped to manage the summer programs, and worked with the fourteen full-gospel churches that were helping with the Olympic rally. I even got some private singing lessons. (Most people who know me would say those lessons did me no good.)

My whole point is this: Two and a half years before this ministry opportunity came along, God had worked in my life in such a way that I developed an ongoing love for holiness, righteousness, and purity, while at the same time developing a hatred for sin. God's ongoing development in my life resulted in the desire to live purely, which prepared me for an increase of the anointing during this pivotal time of my life. The anointing resulted in effectiveness. Effectiveness resulted in opportunity, and opportunity resulted in exaltation. Getting out of school two and half weeks early, and getting paid just about as much as a high school senior as I earn now, can definitely be considered exaltation. All of these things brought joy to my life.

Not many things in life bring our pastors more joy than accomplishing what God has put in their heart to do. Just as pastors come in all shapes and sizes, so do their visions. It is neither my job nor your job to judge their vision. Our desire is to see our pastors accomplish all that is in their hearts. Yet no matter what their vision is, it cannot be accomplished without the anointing.

The anointing will bring your pastor joy. The anointing will help your pastor to accomplish God's will. The anointing allows your pastor to know that God is with him or her in a powerful way. These are certainties every pastor needs. Therefore, let's pray that our pastors will keep their passion for holiness hot and their hatred for sin burning, so they can be anointed with the oil of joy. This special joy comes from completing the will of God and accomplishing the vision burning inside their hearts.

Prayer for Our Pastors

Father, in the name of Jesus I pray for my pastor. I believe that You are going to give him a greater passion for everything that is beautiful in You. I declare in Jesus' name that his passion for holiness, righteousness, and purity is growing ever stronger, and he is developing a perfect hatred for all that is evil and sinful. As a result of this prayer, I believe You will anoint him with Your power, and I believe that the anointing is going to make him effective in everything that is valuable to You, and that accomplishing all that is valuable to You will bring overflowing joy into his life. I believe that You will anoint him to be effective as the leader of our congregation and of his home, and that both will be a joy to his heart. In Jesus' name, Amen!

Chapter 9

The Prosperous Pastor

*All your robes are fragrant with myrrh
and aloes and cassia; from palaces
adorned with ivory the music of the
strings makes you glad.*
(Psalm 45:8)

Not Exactly High Rolling

When I first came to pastor in Cairo, the church had only nine members. It had been without a pastor for a long period of time. This situation is usually not a good indicator of being offered a high-paying ministry position. Yet I was blessed because they had a parsonage for me to live in ... and notice I said a "parsonage," not a house. It was really a shack. The house was probably built in the late 1890's or early 1900's. Luckily for me, the interior had been redecorated sometime in the 70's. The bright lime green vinyl flooring all throughout the house gave that away. The outside of the house had not been painted in decades, and if you ran your hands across the wooden clapboards of the house, chunks of dried paint would fall to the ground covering the earth like snow. I told the church not to bother putting money into the house. My reasoning went as follows: the church was not in much better shape than the house, and most people in the community thought the house was vacant anyway; I knew that if the church did better financially, then I would do better financially as well. Most people did not associate that hideous house with the church property anyway, and so I figured it was better not to even bring up the subject.

For the sole purpose of giving me some relief from the lime green vinyl flooring, I found some carpet to go in the living room. The first piece of carpet did not cover the whole living room floor, so I found another piece to place on the other half of the floor. My living room had beige carpet on one half of the room and pink carpet on the other side of the room. It gets better! The joint in these carpets met by the dining room, and the dining room still had the lime green vinyl. Since I only had a few pieces of furniture, moving in was a cinch. My furniture topped the room off with beauty. I had a good-quality bedroom suite and a nice dining room table. I also had a faded, old, flower-print couch from the early 80's and a bronze orange recliner that would probably have to be carbon dated to find the age. My house was the very definition of ugliness.

You might also remember I had no heat. During my stay in the house, I started having terrible indigestion. Some people suggested that it was the stress of pastoring my first congregation, but that was not the case. The reality was that the floor in my bedroom was not level, and so I was sleeping at an angle with my feet above me head. When I discovered the problem, I placed a brick under each leg of the head side of the bed, and my indigestion was cured.

The night I moved in, my mother said she saw a rat that looked more like cat. I thought she was exaggerating until I saw something unbelievable the next morning. When I saw the loaf of bread I had left on the kitchen counter, it had a hole eaten through it the size of a paper towel roll. The church members informed me that I had a wharf rat, and when I told them I would lay out a trap, they laughed. They said they would bring me a metal cage. The cage never worked. Every time I would catch him, the rat would chew his way out of the cage before I could get to him. I finally put out poison. The poison killed him, but he died in the wall and the smell just about killed me for two months.

My pay was great as well. I told them that if they brought me on full time, then I would be able to make up that salary in three months. My confidence inspired them, and they decided to pay me two hundred dollars a week along with a one hundred dollar a month expense check. They also paid for half my health insurance and half my social security. (Now that I have pastored for a much longer time, God has since placed such youthful self-confidence on the threshing floor and worked much of that out of my life, but in my early years in the ministry that confidence served me well.) I actually thought I was rich because I did not have to pay for the wonderful house I was living in, and because I had just graduated from college. My living accommodations were more like a lateral move from dorm life.

Those were fun days. Realistically, though, the only reason I was able to survive was because dorm life had dulled my senses and desires for the comforts of home, and secondly, because I was single. Not many American women would have lived in such horrible circumstances. Since that time I have increased in financial blessing repeatedly, and I find myself in a place of abundance. Financial stress is still present at times; nevertheless, I have made major strides forward in this area of life.

The Rich-smelling Pastor

The psalmist tells us, *"All your robes are fragrant with myrrh and aloes and cassia; from palaces adorned with ivory the music of the strings makes you glad."* This verse makes an observation about the king, and we should make the same observation about our pastors. The psalmist says the king's robe smells like myrrh, aloes, and cassia. All of these plants were ingredients in perfumes. They were all expensive and they smelled wonderful to people in that culture. This points to the fact that the king was wealthy. The phrase "from palaces of ivory" reinforces this reality. Ivory comes from the tusk of elephants. Ivory was a sign of exotic places of great wealth. The psalmist was noting that the king was wealthy.

The "Poor" Facts

In reality, such observations should be made of our pastors. I will tell you the reason why in just a moment, but for now I want to draw your attention to the fact that "seventy percent of pastors feel grossly underpaid.[15]" The reality is most pastors are certainly not thought of as belonging to the community of the prosperous. Many people in congregations across the nation will joke around by praying this mock prayer, "Lord, if you keep him humble, then we will keep him poor." This is not God's best for your pastor or for your congregation.

The Relation between Wealth and Worship

The psalmist makes a unique observation. He connects the king's wealth with his ability to enjoy and experience worship. It's stated like this: *"The music of the strings makes you glad."* Why is it that the psalmist makes a connection between wealth and worship? The answer is simple if you are a pastor. When a pastor is concerned about money either personally or on behalf of the church, then he is distracted. He is distracted from his most important priority: giving worship and glory to God. It is not that he is unspiritual, or that his worship is super-

---

[15] Maranatha Life's Lifeline for Pastors

ficial. It's just that if he's consumed with money worries, he cannot fully direct his mind to the presence of God. It is almost as if he is attempting to enjoy the music in the sanctuary from another room in the facility. He finds himself removed not just from the music mentally, but also from the presence of God spiritually.

What Does the Bible Teach about Paying the Pastor?

The New Testament is very clear on this point as well. First Timothy 5:17 says, *"The elders who direct the affairs of the church well are worthy of double honor, especially those whose work is preaching and teaching."* I like the plain tone of the New Living Translation in regard to the same verse: *"Elders who do their work well should be paid well, especially those who work hard at both preaching and teaching."* First Corinthians 9:11 is unequivocal as well, *"If we have sown spiritual seed among you, is it too much if we reap a material harvest from you?"* The sad reality is many churches do not enjoy blessing their pastor monetarily, but it is imperative for congregations to learn the importance of this spiritual principle.

The Congregation Benefits from Paying the Pastor Well

Congregants need to learn that blessing their pastor in regard to finances will benefit the entire congregation in many ways. One, it will bring the congregation into obedience with the Word of God, and that will result in financial blessing for the church. Two, it will free the pastor to focus on the affairs of the church because he will not have pressing monetary concerns at home. Three, as our pastor prospers, we prosper, because he is the head of our congregation. The blessing he receives, we receive as well[16]. Four, as the congregation gives more to the pastor, they respect and cherish him or her more. People value what they pay for. Anything that comes cheap, free, or easy does not receive the same measure of importance as something sacrificed for. Do we value the gift of the pastor? The pastor is a gift given by Christ to the church. Our willingness to give to our spiritual leaders shows appreciation, thanksgiving, and value. Our giving to our pastors is not about them in many ways; it is about us. Five, an expansion of wealth can increase time for your pastor. An example might be rather than he cutting his own grass, he is able to pay someone else to cut his lawn. This would free up time for him to spend with his family, on a hobby, or in God's presence. Six, when the pastor shows signs of wealth, it opens doors for him to minister to people of influence within the community. Why should the city council, county commissioners, boards of education, business leaders, and chambers of commerce listen to spiritual leaders who are broke and on the verge of bankruptcy? Finally, having financial peace of mind helps the pastor to engage the presence of God in a

---

[16] Hosea 4:9

totally undistracted manner. This results in a greater unction in his or her ministry. A great anointing can only be cultivated in the presence of God.

Praying Prosperity for Your Pastor

In light of these truths, it is important we pray for the financial well being of our pastors. Some pastors are bi-vocational by necessity. In situations such as these, we need to pray our churches will be able to afford to pay their pastor so they can fully engage their calling. Taking a step of faith into a professional full-time pasturing career at a church should occur without the pastor suffering financially for having made that decision.

Some pastors are bi-vocational by choice or by calling; in this case, we need to pray they prosper at whatever they put their hand to. (The choice to be bi-vocational needs to be rooted in one of the following categories: 1) A calling that enables the pastor to exert greater influence for Christ in their non-ministry career than they could within their ministry career; 2) Their career leads to great financial blessing for the pastor and the congregation; or 3) The pastor feels this enables him to pastor the church more effectively.)

Many pastors are in what is called "full-time ministry," yet they are suffering for that decision financially. This should not be the case. Our desire needs to be for our pastor to prosper. We need to exercise diligence in praying for the congregation's ability to pay our pastors well. Our prayers also need to be with those in positions of authority. Asking God to give them a generous spirit will result in their willingness to pay the pastor increasing amounts as the church is blessed.

If we could truly take hold of this spiritual principle, it would revolutionize our congregations.

Prayer for Our Pastor's Prosperity

Father, I come to You in the name of Jesus,
Your strong and glorious son. I come asking
that my pastor will be blessed financially.
Let him not only be blessed in his finances,
but also let there not even be a hint of
poverty in his life. I ask that the very smell
of prosperity will radiate from him, and
that he will carry himself in a manner that
exudes the dignity and confidence that only
comes from Your blessing. This dignity
and confidence will give him the means to
minister to the rich and to the poor. Father,
I also ask that there will not be anything in
his personal life that will distract him from
coming into Your presence, and that during
the times when he is seeking You in worship,
he will be able to give You his full attention.
I also ask that the financial blessing on his
life will multiply his time, therefore giving
him more opportunity to spend time in Your
presence.

Section 2

Praying for Your Pastor's Wife

Chapter 10

The Honored Pastor's Wife

*Daughters of kings are among your
honored women; at your right hand is the
royal bride in gold of Ophir. Listen, O
daughter, consider and give ear: Forget
your people and your father's house. The
king is enthralled by your beauty; honor
him, for he is your lord.*
(Psalm 45:9-11)

An Unexpected Meeting

I clearly remember the day when I first spotted my wife. I had traveled to South Carolina to buy some tables and chairs for our church from another congregation. I had borrowed an old Chevy S-10 truck from a friend, and it had no air conditioning. The trip home was on a hot summer day, and every mile south I drove, it grew hotter. One of my young deacons, who had just graduated from college, was getting married in Dublin, Georgia. Dublin was at the halfway point of the trip, but as I got closer I got sweatier and hotter. My motivation to stop and clean up to attend the wedding began to wane.

I was actually considering not interrupting the trip for the wedding, but as I came to the outskirts of Dublin, I also came to my senses. The reality of pastoral obligation put my feet back on the ground, and I was running late. Nevertheless, I called ahead and the groom's family had a key waiting for me at their hotel room. I quickly showered, changed clothes, and headed to the wedding. When I arrived, I sat toward the front of the church along with one of the groom's relatives.

I had barely sat down when the wedding processional began. The bridesmaids started down the aisle. One walked down the aisle … the second one came through the door and started her trek down the aisle … and then when the third bridesmaid began walking down the aisle, it was like the lights of heaven were shining down on her! I even thought I heard angels singing as I watched the most beautiful girl in the whole world coming down the aisle. I was so gripped with emotion I released the most profound statement that came to mind: "Whoa, Momma!"

I leaned over to my friend and said, "I am going to talk to her after the wedding."

He said, "Down, boy."

After the wedding, I lingered in the sanctuary while the photographs were being taken. I did this so I could "check out" this girl. I stood in the back of the church making small talk with people. I was attempting to see if anyone in the back had any relationship with the girl. I asked a few people who they were with and how they were related to the bride and groom. I eventually hit the jackpot. I ran into the girl's father. The family, amazingly, used to live in Cairo, the town where I now lived. I discovered where they used to go to church, how long they had served the Lord, the ministry she was actively participating in, and where she presently attended church. I asked about their family heritage in serving the Lord. I had found the gold at the end of the rainbow. Now I just had to meet her.

When they had finished taking pictures, she came down the steps on the right side of the platform and starting walking down the outside aisle. I somehow managed to make my way in that direction. The girl looked at me and said, "Hey!" My heart stopped, but she kept walking.

I found my way to the reception hall at the nearby civic club. I had to ask some of the members in the wedding party to introduce me to the beautiful bridesmaid. I was ready to meet her. I asked my friend Jim to introduce us. His answer took me back; he flat-out said, "No!" I was very disheartened at his response.

I walked over to watch the bride dancing with her father. I felt someone standing close behind me, so I turned around suddenly and there was Jim and the beautiful bridesmaid. He said, "Cameron, this is Rachel." Then he totally disappeared. I started talking to her, asking about her testimony, what college she went to, her major, her interests, her grades, her friends, and her theology. I asked her about pretty much everything you could ever want to know about a person! About the only things I did not do were take a blood sample and ask for her transcripts. Then the DJ called everyone out onto the dance floor. This presented me with three problems. One, in my church tradition we do not dance, and the fact that my deacon was having dancing at his wedding was borderline scandalous with many of his older relatives. Two, I do not dance. I have the rhythm of a cow. Three, I did not know if Rachel would be comfortable dancing with me. Therefore, I did the logical thing and asked her to dance. It was glorious! At the end of the dance, I had broken no bones in her feet, and she was willing to give me her phone number. In six months we were engaged, and a year to the date we were married.

Since that time Rachel has become my right arm in ministry and in life. She is my best friend. Whether we're in each other's arms or riding around town, she is the one I discuss my life and dreams with. She encourages me when I am down, and conversely, when things are going well, it is her input that is the most meaningful to me. I can have a hundred people tell me I preached great on Sunday, but her compliment is the only one that excites me deep in my heart.

Bless Her Too

In the process of praying for our pastor, we also must keep his wife in prayer[17]. Most pastors consider their home life to be sacred, and pastors can only be effective when love, joy, and peace are flowing in their home.

The palmist does not leave the bride out of the blessing. He includes the new queen in his prayer. Just as his blessing is relevant to the Shepherd of Israel's wife, it will be a blessing to the shepherd of our congregation's wife as well. The psalmist gives the reader a brief and simple guide that can serve as a wonderful outline for prayer.

Her Influence

The writer starts his blessing with the following, *"Daughters of kings are among your honored women."* We know in the immediate context he is talking about the bridal party in the wedding. It usually consists of the bride's closest friends. Let's take a look at who these close friends are. They are "daughters of kings." This woman associates with people of influence and accomplishment.

This points to an important aspect of praying for your pastor's wife. Many have heard the statement, "You cannot associate with turkeys and fly with

[17] The spouse of a minister does not have to be a woman (in other words, the minister might be a woman and thus her spouse is her husband), but the text suggests that it is, so we are following the logic of the text.

eagles." We desire our pastor's wife to associate with eagles. I know it is hard to believe, but there are a few politically minded people in the church. Many of these political people will attempt to get close to the pastor's wife so they can influence the pastor. Generally, this drains the pastor's wife because shallow relationships are not fulfilling. A healthy pastor's wife develops relationships in which she can soar with friends she can connect with on a deep, personal level.

This is not the sole reason she needs to be with women of influence. One of the responsibilities of leadership is to influence others who also possess influence. This increases the amount of influence the pastor and his wife have in the church and in the community. Pastors that have a vision for community transformation need to have wives that can influence the influencers.

Her Friends

It is also important for the pastor's wife to have real, true friends of her own. So many people in the church get jealous if the pastor has some people he is closer to than others. In many cases, the cruelty of jealousy does not affect the pastor, but it really hurts his wife. So many pastors' wives are in bondage at church, because if she talks to one person then another person is mad she did not talk to them. If she goes to see a movie with one group of friends, then another person that was not invited is offended. This bondage strips pastors' wives from connecting with close friends on an intimate level and can force them into a shallow mode of relating with everyone on a superficial level. This is not biblical or healthy, and it can create resentment toward the church on her part. Praying believers must break the power of jealousy that would attempt to control, manipulate, and intimidate the pastor's wife. The pastor's wife must be free to connect with real friends who are her caliber spiritually and emotionally.

Understanding and Praying for Her Primary Mission

The psalmist then states, *"At your right hand is the royal bride in gold of Ophir."* She is at the pastor's side, and she is looking good while doing it. Many people do not realize what the primary ministry of the pastor's wife is. It is not to plan the potluck dinners. It is not to head up the women's ministry. It is not to run the nursery or to play the piano. The primary calling of the pastor's wife is to minister to her husband. This is priority number one in her ministry, and if that is all she does, then the congregation needs to be okay with that. In the natural it is impossible, but when God's people are praying, the first lady can be freed of all expectations that would prevent her from accomplishing her primary mission.

Family Matters

The next phrase is a unique statement. *"Listen, O daughter, consider and give ear: Forget your people and your father's house."* We know that our pastor's wife is not exempt from "honoring her father and mother.[18]" So, what does this mean? How can this help us pray for our pastor's wife? I think this points to three things: homesickness, family distractions that hinder the ministry, and baggage from the past.

Homesickness

Many Sunday afternoons we come home from church, park in our carport, and look over at our next-door neighbor's house. Our neighbors have grown children and tons of grandchildren, and most Sundays after church all the kids go to their parents' house for lunch. There are kids and grandkids running around the house and yard. We often look at our daughter and think, "I wish your grandparents could see you all dressed up." Then we imagine how a roast at Momma's house sure would be great right now. Rachel then wishes her brothers were closer, and we comment about how we wish we lived closer to our families.

The nature of ministry is that it takes you away from family[19]. Jesus acknowledged this reality. Yet, in many cases this is much harder on the spouse of

---

[18] Exodus 20:12
[19] Luke 14:26

the pastor. The pastor is usually driven by passion, vision, and dreams. These generally consume him or her, but the spouse might not feel these desires quite as fervently. Often the desire to be with family stings a little more for her. We need to pray for the pastor's wife that God will comfort her and will remove the pain of homesickness from her heart.

Distracted by Family Problems

The pastor's wife can be discouraged if her parents and/or siblings are going through difficult times and she can't be with them. The problem is compounded when these feelings of discouragement are coupled with homesickness, being located so far away that it requires a plane flight to get to her family, and practical obstacles that prevent her from intervening closely. This toxic combination then leads to a huge attack of guilt. Even if she were not a pastor's wife, when a woman lives far away from her parents and problems are happening with them, she can't just hop up and go, but adult daughters naturally feel this strong tug on their hearts to be there. The vast majority of pastors' spouses are women, and women usually have a nurturing instinct that kicks in when problems occur. If this attack on the pastor's relatives is effective at impacting the whole family and congregation, then the enemy is more likely to continue to cause problems in the extended family. This results in the minister's home being out of balance, thus robbing the peace from the home life of the minister and his spouse. Congregations must pray for protection and peace over the extended families of the minister and his wife.

Baggage from the Past

Not every pastor or pastor's wife comes from a strong Christian home. In reality, many pastors emerge from dysfunctional families. This can create baggage in the life of the minister and his wife. This baggage affects the home and ministry of the entire family. The wife is usually concerned about the atmosphere in the home, and this is why she needs your prayers. In this sense both partners *"need to forget your people, and your father's house."* In light of this, we need to ask God to free our pastors from baggage that will attempt to influence their home, their marriage, and their service of the ministering couple.

The Stoker of the Fire

We have all heard the terrible stories about ministers who've had moral failures. Many of these failures are in the realm of sexuality, which often shocks people to learn because they believe their pastor is not concerned about sex. Shocking as it may be, the pastor is probably more concerned about sex than the average person. A minister is passionate, emotional, and filled with desire, goals, and vision. Passion isn't only released when they are preaching, equipping, praying, or serving. This passion is derived from reservoirs deep within their souls, and it flows into all areas of their life. At the same time, the pace of ministry is tiresome and long. Besides these realities, you throw in the fact that many ministers work closely with others on deep, intimate, and personal levels, and that they are under greater demonic attack than most people. Under these circumstances it becomes obvious that adultery is a real danger to the minister. The enemy tempts pastors to allow the fountain of passion for ministry to spill over into the desires of the flesh such as gluttony or sexual sin. We usually think of ministers as the most unlikely to have an affair, but in reality they can be the most tempted.[20]

In light of this reality, the psalmist makes this statement, *"The king is enthralled by your beauty."* There is a grace that can come upon a man's wife that can keep him mystified. The psalmist is not making an indictment against the king's or the pastor's character. He is just blessing his wife with the ability to keep him mystified. He is praying that she will stay the focus of his attention and the object of his passion. He is praying that she will help divorce-proof their marriage.[21]

---

[20] Pastor Randy Valimont taught on this principle during my Pastoral Theology class in college. I have found this to be consistent with my life and with the life of many other pastors.

[21] I am in no way implying it is the pastor's wife's responsibility to keep him out of sexual sin. It is the minister's sole responsibility to walk before the Lord in purity. Yet, this daunting task is much easier when passion is present in the home between the pastor and his wife.

When Rachel and I were expecting our first child, Rachel was busy preparing for the baby. One of the things she was most concerned about was a new concept to me. She called it "baby-proofing the house." When we baby-proofed the house, we put plastic covers on the electrical outlets to keep the baby from shocking herself. We put locks on the cabinet doors to keep her from getting into the poisonous cleaning agents we had in the house. We also cut the strings on the blinds so the baby could not strangle herself. We even bought gates so we could contain the baby in certain areas of the house. We did everything we could to see that the house was baby-proofed. However, none of this guaranteed the prevention of harm to the baby in the house. It was simply proof that we had attempted to be thorough in our responsibilities as parents. We understood if we did our part, the chance the baby would be hurt in our house would not be eliminated, but it would be reduced.

The psalmist is blessing the king's wife with the ability to "adultery-proof" the house. This "adultery-proofing" does not provide a total guarantee that infidelity will be prevented in the marriage. Nonetheless, it is the grace of God to the pastor's wife to be diligent in doing her part in protecting the marriage. This grace does not manifest in the form of nagging and suspicion. Such behavior is counterproductive, and actually isolates the pastor even further away from the arms of his wife. The special grace that is spoken of in this prayer is for the pastor's wife to keep her husband mesmerized, thus causing him to return to her arms with total satisfaction.

As a member of your pastor's congregation, you need to pray God will grace your pastor's wife with the ability to "adultery-proof" their marriage. You need to pray the pastor will only have eyes for his wife, and his wife by her mystique and creativity will constantly take hold of her man's heart.

Honor

Men don't need love in a marriage; they need honor and respect. If they have those two things, then they will have all the love they can handle. Pastors need a double dose of honor, because so many times they are dishonored by people in the congregation. Sometimes a pastor gives his best to a service, a function, or an event, only to have a loud but small minority complain, criticize, and gripe about his best efforts and the best efforts of his team. This leads to discouragement and frustration, but if the man of God is not honored at home, then it just adds insult to injury. The psalmist realized the Shepherd of Judah needed to be honored. That is why he exhorted the new queen to *"honor him, for he is your lord."*

Men of God need respect and honor. The congregation needs to pray for the pastor's wife, asking that she will be anointed to give honor in such a way that it will build self-esteem and give him courage to fight another day. It is an incredible task ministering to the man of God, but with the help of the prayers of the saints, she can minister to his needs in a powerful and effective way.

Reaping Honor

While the pastor's wife is sowing the seeds of honor by revering her husband, she should also reap in receiving honor from the congregation. The psalmist allows the reader to understand this woman is to be respected. The reaping should come from the church and the world. He states it like this: *"The Daughter of Tyre will come with a gift, men of wealth will seek your favor."* The favor on her life not only occurs within the church, but also emerges from outside the church. The daughter of Tyre even comes to honor her with a gift.

Tyre was the capital city of the Phoenician people located to the north of Israel. They were a mercantile people who sailed the Mediterranean Sea with immense proficiency. The new queen even received the honor of this very rich, prosperous, but pagan nation. The blessing of favor on her life gave her influence, answers, and authority. This resulted in the great influencers of their time seeking out her blessing and her graces.

Should the people of God settle for anything less than the magnitude of this blessing resting on their pastor's wife? For her to blossom into the calling that graces her with influence and authority, she must be raised up in prayer. Without your prayers she may never step into the calling of grace and favor this scripture beckons her to, but this calling is not hers to bear alone. It is the calling of the congregation to cover her in grace and favor, so she can distribute the gifts lavished on her during your times of prayer. Just as Jesus grew in favor with man, so can this lady of style, poise, and beauty[22]. The call on your life is to never criticize her, but to bountifully cover her in your prayers so the blessing of God can rest on your life.

A Prayer for the Pastor's Wife

Dear Heavenly Father, I come to You in the name of Jesus praying for my pastor's wife. I pray that You will bless her with true and close friends in our congregation, and as she experiences these friendships, I ask that the power of all jealousy will be broken in our congregation concerning this matter, and she will be free of all feelings of condemnation that have attempted to come on her about this matter of relationships. I pray that her friends will be people of influence – increasing her influence in the community and in the church, and that her friends will challenge her to new heights and new levels in maturity and in intimacy with You. I also ask that she will be free to accomplish her primary call – the call to her husband – and she will be anointed to meet his needs. I declare in Jesus' name that all unbiblical

---

[22] Luke 2:52

*and unrealistic expectations are removed
from her spirit, soul, and body. I believe with
Your grace she will only endeavor to accomplish the will of God and not the will of man.
Father, I also pray that if she is homesick in
any way, You will be her comfort and peace.
I ask that You will bless her family and keep
them from harm, and during times of trial,
I ask that she will be in complete peace and
faith knowing her family is in Your hands.
I also pray for her and Pastor's marriage,
and if there is any baggage from their past
– especially from their family – I ask that
you will heal their hurts and grant repen-
tance of any behaviors that influence their
marriage in a negative manner.
I request you strengthen their marriage, and
that pastor will only have eyes for his wife,
and his wife by her mystique and creativity
will constantly take hold of his heart.
I also request she will have a special grace
to honor him. I believe that every time he
is discouraged or has been dishonored, she
will lift him up with words and actions that
communicate honor and respect toward him.
Anoint her to build his self-esteem when the
world and the enemy attempt to tear him
down. In light of this, I also ask just as she
has sown in honoring her husband, she will
also reap in honor a hundred times over. The
people inside and outside the church will
cherish and respect her. I declare in Jesus'*

name that all people will see the favor on her life and that they will seek the blessings of that favor. In Jesus' name, Amen!

Section 3

How to Pray for Your Pastor's Children

Chapter 11

The Glorious Daughter

All glorious is the princess within her chamber; her gown is interwoven with gold. In embroidered garments she is led to the king; her virgin companions follow her and are brought to you. They are led in with joy and gladness; they enter the palace of the king.
(Psalm 45:13-15)

The Loud One

My daughter was opinionated from the moment she was born. She is not one who struggles making a decision or even making a choice for others. Even before she was fully born, her ear-piercing screams shook the hospital doors. In terms of her volume level, she has entirely taken after her father. She knows what she desires, and when she does not receive her wishes, she is not shy about reminding any person there is something missing. Even from infancy, my daughter has reflected in her disposition the desire to be with her father. In times past when I have busily run around attempting to accomplish great feats for God in contrast to spending adequate amounts of time with my daughter, she has let me know. When I finally would spend time with her, she would act distant toward me. She would shun me like a teenage girl who is silently angry at her boyfriend, but as I reinvested in our relationship, she began to come alive with the joy of a father's love. After the shunning has stopped and my investment has been made, our time is filled with giggles, tickles, and funny faces.

My daily prayer for my daughter is that I will have her affections until she is married, and then "he will have her affections." My desire is that my daughter and I will always be close. One of the utmost tragedies in ministers' lives is when they endeavor to save their world, but lose their kids in the process. My life would be a waste if I won the whole world for Jesus, but lost my kids.

The kingdom of darkness is well aware of the fact that many ministers, filled with zeal for the church and their Lord, can give the impression to their children that their acts of service are more important than their relationship with them. In the midst of this chaos, the enemy is rapid to move in and whisper fabrications in their ears that reinforce this falsehood. He is endeavoring to pave the way for prodigal children to be lost in the prison of rebellion, locked in by the keys of bitterness and rejection. This scheme of the enemy can be cancelled and negated if the people of God will rise up and pray for the pastor's family.

Five Prayers

In these verses, the psalmist utters the prayer of blessing for the king's daughter. Understand that if the king's whole family is not blessed, then the king himself is not blessed. Many people pray for their pastor, interceding that the blessing of God will rest upon him, but if his family relationships are not strong, then he will not be blessed at all. In light of this wisdom, we must align ourselves with the psalmist by praying for our spiritual leader's family and in this case his daughter. The psalmist gives us five specific things we can pray over our pastor's daughter or daughters.

Pray that the Pastor's Daughter Will Radiate Glory

The psalmist declares, *"All glorious is the princess within her chamber."* The daughter of the pastor is to be filled with joy and intimacy with God, not just in public where she might be expected to put on a show, but even in her own room—the room where so many pastors' daughters hide their depression and secretly whisper curses at the ministry. But that's not the case in this prayer. She is glorious within her chambers. This joy radiates on her face, and it is rooted not in regurgitated religion, but in a deep personal and real relationship with God. This relationship is not just leftovers from her parent's religion that result in a superficial connection with a distant creator. This relationship is not experienced on the platform of public performance. It is engaged and activated in the privacy of her own chamber. The glory that overshadows this pastor's daughter is cultivated in private and radiated in public. She is not depressed about her lot in life during the secret watches of the night, but she is delighted that she is alone with her Savior. Should the people of God believe for anything less for the daughters of their pastor? Our prayer is that pastors' daughters will be, "All glorious ... within their chamber."

Pray that the Pastor's Daughter Will Prosper

Many children grow up in families with parents working numerous hours. My mother would work ten to twelve-hour days at the post office. My father was a carpenter who worked for a construction company that contracted with insurance companies conducting restoration work on burned houses, and after his regular work hours, he always had side jobs lined up as a secondary source of income. During the summer he also farmed on our small farm in Pelzer, South Carolina. Hard work and long hours were the norm in our household when I was growing up. It was not unusual to have one or both parents work sixty hours a week. This is common for many families across the United States.

In spite of this common reality among all working parents, if a person talks to pastors' kids across the nation, and if dad works a forty-five to fifty-hour week just once a month, then "Dad loves the ministry more than me." Pastors' kids commonly say things like, "I hate the ministry" ... "I hate the church" ... "I am never going to church when I get older, or if I do I will not be really committed to it." Both of my parents worked substantially more than I do, but I never said, "I hate the post office; when I grow up I'm never going to mail a letter. All of my bills are going to be drafted out of my bank account because I don't want to support the post office." I have never said, "I hate the construction business; I don't even want to live in a house because the construction business takes daddies away from their kids." In reality, the opposite of both statements is true. I send all of my bills through the post office because I desire to support the entity that gave my mom a good job and thereby increased the quality of my life. Whenever I need to make some quick cash, I will do a construction project with my limited skills. If I think of children who have parents who work long hours in professions other than the ministry, they are not upset about the matter. I have never met the child of a doctor who was extremely unhappy being a doctor's child. I have never met one who said, "When I get sick, I am never going to a hospital when I grow up, because hospitals take parents away from their children."

A thinking person has to ask, "What's the difference?" There are two differences. First, the pastor and his family are under enhanced demonic attack. This has to be the reason such a vast group of pastors' children tends to make such rash and illogical conclusions about their parents' vocation. The second difference is prosperity. When my parents worked longer hours, I reaped immediate benefits in the form of more toys, great vacations, and going out to eat more often.

In most professions, the more you work, the more you make. This leads to an immediate benefit to the children and the family. This is not normally true for the ministry. In many churches, the pastor works sixty hours a week for peanuts. His family cannot afford to go out to eat. They are shopping at thrift stores. They cannot go on vacations that have the combination of comfort and length. So in reality, the benefit of working long hours is removed from the position. In light of this, the children begin to view the ministry as a curse. "If those people are going to take my parents from me by working them to death, then they can at least pay them enough to take us on a vacation or to go to a nice restaurant once a week." I personally believe this issue can grate on a girl in a slightly different way than a boy, and that is why I have listed it in this section of the book concerning prayers for the pastor's daughter.

In the case of the king's daughter, her clothing is interwoven with gold. She prospers because her father is the king. Should it be any different if her father is a pastor? No! She should be blessed because her father is prospering the ministry, and as the ministry prospers, they in turn prosper him. We should pray the minister's daughter would not be deprived because of the ministry. A religious spirit is welling up in some people who are reading this right now and thinking, *well, if the minister has chosen the work of the ministry, then he should be willing to sacrifice*. The problem is his daughter was born into the ministry, not called into the ministry, and whatever sacrifices have to be made due to the ministry can be made with greater ease if his daughter is well taken care of financially.

Pray She Will Have a Open Relationship with Her Father

The princess in this psalm is *"led to the King."* The king surely has important matters to employ, but none are more significant than his daughter. We need to call upon the Lord that the pastor's daughters will have the sentiment that nothing church related is more significant to their father than his relationship with her.

Often when I am working at the house or taking care of some family business, my daughter walks up to me, pats me on the knee and says, "Daddy, lap!" At that point, nothing is more essential than my daughter. My lap is reserved for her whenever she wants it.

There are many things that can hinder the father-daughter relationship: busyness, unspoken hurts, other priorities, neglect or just being out of the cultural loop. But in the case of the king and the princess, there was an open and honest relationship. This needs to be prayed over in every father-daughter relationship, but in the case of the pastor-daughter relationship, this is even more imperative. Sometimes the pastor's passionate personality can intimidate the child, or there might be an unspoken feeling that the daughter needs to have it all together due to the fact she is "the pastor's daughter." So to make sure these misconceptions and lies never take root, God's people must gird up the pastor and his daughter in prayer believing God their relationship will be intimate, real, and transparent.

Pray She Will Be Surrounded by Good Company

The Bible says that, "Bad company corrupts good character."[23] This is true of all relationships, but look at the group the princess runs with: "her virgin companions follow her." The princess runs with virgins. Yes, this can be the standard for your children's friends even in a time when one out of four teens in America has a sexually transmitted disease.[24] If the pastor's family is going to stay strong, then his daughters need friends who are clean and fun. If you want your pastor's daughter to come into her godly calling, then she needs some godly friends.

---

[23] 1 Corinthians 15:33

[24] Sarah   Forhan,   www.cdc.gov/stdconference/2008/media/
summaries-11march2008.htm#tues1

Pray She and Her Friends Will Be Close to the Family

Due to the work ethic of my parents, we had a boat and a lake house. The lake house was a good reason for my friends to come around. It was a lot easier to stay out of trouble when my friends wanted to be with my parents and me. Luckily, my parents allowed me to fill our house with friends on a regular basis. It was a great place to play and relax, and they allowed my friends to do that as well. My parents wisely had the same philosophy of parenting as the king had. Verse 15 tells us that, *"They are led in with joy and gladness; they enter the palace of the king."* The king's daughter and her virgin friends are all close to her family. They are able to connect and experience life and love together.

I had a friend in high school whose parents lived in a huge house. The only problem was the decor. It was decorated with everything fine, expensive, and easily breakable. My friend's parents were serious people. Nevertheless, they believed they were fun people to be around. Sadly, no one else did. They were the type of people who stared at you over their bifocals if you were having too much fun. I detested being at their house. You never felt you could be yourself. It was like being in prison. The pastor's home needs to be a refuge for his family. It should be a place of joy and gladness not only for the nuclear family, but also for the friends of the children. These things can be a reality if God's people are willing to lift up their pastor in prayer.

Prayer for the Pastor's Daughter

Father, I come to You on behalf of _____
_____, my pastor's daughter, and I ask
in the name of Jesus that _____ will
radiate the glory of God. I pray her life
will be filled with real joy, the kind that is
genuine in public but is rooted in private;
joy that is satisfied in all of life, even when
she is alone. I also ask that her relation-
ship with You will be intimate and real
with nothing fake or false. Protect her from
religion that denies the power of God, but
bask her in Your glorious presence until
her whole life is a splendid reflection of
You. Free her from any pressure to perform
under the gazes of self-righteous people who
do not know or understand her, and would
ignorantly attempt to put her in their box. I
thank You, God, that this glory is going to be
cultivated in the secret place of her private
sanctuary.
Lord, I also pray You will prosper her, and
she will not experience any lack due to the
ministry. I pray that she will be blessed
because of it. Father, I thank You she is
going to enjoy almost everything about the
ministry, and the parts she does not enjoy
will be manageable due to her prosperity
of spirit, emotion, body, and wallet. In the
name of Jesus, I also request that the rela-
tionship she has with her father will always

be honest, open, and transparent. I thank You that the person she loves to talk to the most is her father, and that Pastor will be anointed to love his daughter in a way that communicates unconditional love. I thank You his door is always open to her, and she knows his welcome is always extended to her. I believe there will never be a wall between them. We bless her with godly friends who will serve as a barrier of protection around her, and that people who will lift her up and walk at her level will be near to her. I thank You that You are going to protect her and her friends from sexual sin, and that her self-esteem would not be found in boys, but in the awareness of who You made her to be. I also request that _____ and her friends will love to be with pastor and his wife. I bless their home as a place their children's friends will always love to be. Let it be a place of fun, fellowship, and laughter. Let it be a place where memories are made, strength is gained, and rejuvenation is the natural byproduct. I thank You for all of these things in Jesus' name, Amen.

Chapter 12

The Influential Son

Your sons will take the place of your fathers;
you will make them princes throughout the
land. I will perpetuate your memory through
all generations; therefore the nations will
praise you for ever and ever.
(Psalm 45:16-17)

Discovering Nowhere

I remember when I first drove into Cairo. Growing up I had always said, "If you cannot get somewhere on an interstate, then I don't want to go." I soon ate those words, because my first trip to Cairo resulted in traveling further off the interstate than I had ever been in my life. I took a labyrinth of state and county roads that were carved through miles of farmland. I finally arrived on the island of Cairo; this island was not surrounded by oceans or seas, but never-ending fields of corn, peanuts, cotton, and soybeans. When I finally turned onto the first US highway I had seen in what felt like an eternity, I was happy to spot a Wal-mart to my left. I thought, *I can live anywhere there is a Wal-mart.* I then looked to my right and saw a Dairy Queen. I considered to myself, *I not only can live here, I can thrive here!* There is not too much better in life than a hand-dipped ice cream cone after a wonderful day of Sunday church services. I traveled a few more blocks to 5th Street where I turned right, and then I saw the church building. The moment I saw it I said, "Oh my God, that is it." I did not say it because I was happy, or because I felt the Holy Spirit confirming in my heart this was the place I was to spend the next decade of my life. I said it because it was so ugly and unkempt.

It looked like a traditional church you might see in a Norman Rockwell Painting – but this one looked like it had been crossbred with a barn. It had no steeple. If it had not been for the sign, the average person would have never known it was a church as they went driving by.

I believed God had called me to pastor this church, but I also knew that bringing it up to a standard of excellence would certainly be a daunting task. Not because of the facilities, but due to my understanding that the natural explains the spiritual. If this congregation was living at this shoddy level of excellence in the natural realm, then what level of excellence were they presently living at spiritually?

Steady Progress

When I became the pastor of the congregation, I discovered the nine people who were keeping the church afloat were ready for a change. That made things easier, but it was still a tough challenge. The church needed to be painted on the inside and the outside, so that is where we began our remodeling because it was cheap and did wonders for the facility.

The second big project the church took on after I arrived was the parking lot. At that time, the church did not have a paved parking lot. It just had a red clay plot of land where people parked. So when it rained, it turned into a South Georgia red mud hole. It was a great place to spin your tires and ruin your Sunday shoes. We saved as much money as we could, held fundraisers, and took bids. We did not have all the money we needed, but we took a step of faith and the contractor gave us a deal. We successfully paved the parking lot.

Not much time had passed when we discovered our foundation was rotten and the church was starting to slant to the south. We did not have the money to repair it, but we prayed and gave to missions. We were still short, but God sent a miracle check in the mail, and the foundation was fixed. The church had speakers, but the soundboard was on the platform. It needed to be moved to the back of the sanctuary and put into a sound room – which also needed to be built. We acted and God provided.

One Sunday when I was preaching, I almost fell through the floor. The platform was rotten and a huge hole had developed behind the pulpit. If the twenty-five-year-old carpet had been any weaker, I would have gone through the church floor to the foundation. We ripped out the platform and put in a new one. That platform was the first sign of excellence in our church. The rest of the church still looked like a barn, but that platform looked like it belonged on Broadway. We then redecorated the inside of our sanctuary with new carpet, new paint, and new chairs. The inside of our sanctuary was beautiful. Progress continued, and our congregation eventually relocated to our present facility situated on fifteen acres with a state-of-the-art building. This is truly miraculous when you consider that our congregation is in one of the poorest regions in the United States, coupled with the fact that our church's primary mission is to the poor of our area. The spirit of excellence was starting to come alive in our congregation.

The process of progression and realized goals are things every pastor has his heart set on. This quest for progress and always moving forward to see goals being met would certainly be an eternal waste if spiritual progression failed to occur within the minister's family, especially to his sons.

The Importance of the Son

Currently, my wife and I are believing God for a son as we stand on the promises of the Word of God; the fulfillment of this dream is in the hands of God.

Nevertheless, even if we do not have a son, there are thousands of pastors across the nation that do have sons, and their sons need our prayers.

The psalmist understood this in an even greater light, because one of the king's sons would succeed him as king. I understand that succession of leadership based on the family line does not take place in most churches, but the concept of spiritual succession should be on the forefront of our minds whether we are a pastor or not. If the pastor's call is to equip the saints, then how much more should he equip his children to be skillful and effective leaders and ministers? The children of the pastor have the potential to be the "special forces" of the next generation. These "special forces" are to destroy the works of the devil and establish the Kingdom of God. The pastor's effectiveness at equipping his sons is going to be increased as the congregation intercedes for this inner-family ministry. The four points the psalmist gives us is the guide to enhancing our pastor's call to equip his sons. We are to intercede on behalf of our pastors' sons in these four areas. These prayers are fundamental keys to turning pastor's sons into God's warriors—His "special forces."

Pray the Pastor's Son Will Become a Spiritual Leader

The psalmist said it like this: *"Your sons will take the place of your fathers."* I am not saying you should project the call of ministry on every son of the pastor, but I am saying that spiritual leadership should not be lost from one generation to the next. In truth, it should only increase from generation to generation. This is the prayer request that we should make for the sons of the pastor. Sons should be equipped by the example and at the hand of their father. This equipping should result in the increase of spiritual leadership, regardless of which career field our pastor's children choose to follow. Spiritual leadership is needed in government, business, education, public service, the arts, and the church. We need deacons, elders, pastors, and teachers who will provide leadership within the church. To limit the role of the pastor's son to the professional ministry is to limit God. Nonetheless, spiritual leadership is imperative. The sons should take the places of their fathers. The psalmist saw that the king was prosperous, progressive, and powerful. If this influence died with the king, then the king's rule would ultimately result in failure. In our times of prayer for our pastor, we need to pray that his lineage will continue to grow and expand its influence in the world.

Pray the Pastor's Son Will Presently become a Great Spiritual Leader

The present influence of the pastor's son should be growing wide and deep. *"You will make them princes throughout the land."* This is certainly what the writer had in mind for the children of the king.

We need to agree with the concept that the pastor's sons will receive the spiritual heritage of their father. They need not fall further away from God, but only fall closer to Him in greater faith, dependence, and love. This is not just for the future; it is for the present as well. The pastor's princes need to be *"princes throughout the land."* They need to be leaders within the kingdom of God. Therefore, at the present time the pastor's sons are bringing spiritual leadership to football teams, bands, debate teams, honor clubs, colleges, rodeos, or wherever they find themselves in the moment. The role of the parishioner is not to judge the pastor's sons, but to lift them up in prayer, escorting them in the spirit to the sphere of influence God has prepared for them to walk in. Regardless of the successes in the church, if the pastor's family fails to pass on his heritage, then he will have fallen short of his potential. The growth and expansion of this heritage should not start at the death of the pastor, but at the birth of his sons.

Pray the Pastor's Son Receives His Inheritance from His Father

In terms of inheritance, I am not just talking about monetary possessions, though that is scriptural[25]. I am talking about a spiritual inheritance. The son should not have to go through all of the difficulties and trials his father went through in order to learn the same lessons. He should learn by his father's

---

[25] Proverbs 13:22

example. Where his father's ceiling is in terms of spiritual growth, spiritual gifts, leadership ability, wisdom, perception, talent, and understanding, this should be the floor for the son. The son should be a few rungs higher on the ladder than his father or mother. He should have the ability to climb higher because of the influence of his father. If this takes place, then not only will the son be praised, but the father who trained him will be praised as well, and his memory will last throughout generations to come. This is the primary goal in prayers for our pastor and his family. This was the concluding blessing of the psalmist: *"I will perpetuate your memory through all generations; therefore the nations will praise you for ever and ever."*

Prayer for the Pastor's Son

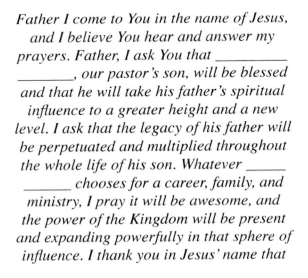

Father I come to You in the name of Jesus, and I believe You hear and answer my prayers. Father, I ask You that _____ _____, our pastor's son, will be blessed and that he will take his father's spiritual influence to a greater height and a new level. I ask that the legacy of his father will be perpetuated and multiplied throughout the whole life of his son. Whatever _____ _____ chooses for a career, family, and ministry, I pray it will be awesome, and the power of the Kingdom will be present and expanding powerfully in that sphere of influence. I thank you in Jesus' name that

*the spiritual house of my pastor is going
to expand and grow stronger through his
son. I also ask that _____ will
presently begin to step into the calling of
spiritual influence that is already on his life.
I ask that wherever the pastor's son is, he
is rising up to a place of influence and he
is becoming a ruling prince in the kingdom
in that location. I thank You that peers or
skeptics would not influence him negatively,
but that instead he is the primary influencer
within his network of relationships. I declare
his influence to be positive, godly, and holy.
Lord, I pray _____ will receive
all his father can give him, and that his
starting point will be his father's ending
point. His father's ceiling will become his
floor. I thank You there is not one area of
his life that is not going to be developed for
Your glory. In Jesus' name, Amen.*

Afterword

The president of the United States is the head of the executive branch of our government. One of the major functions of the presidency is to protect the American people. This role is carried out in many ways, but it is carried out primarily as commander-in-chief. Nevertheless, just because the president's role is to protect the American people, it would be foolish to conclude the president does not need to be protected personally. The president is protected by the Secret Service. So as the president protects us, he is also being protected. My prayer is that God will raise up a spiritual secret service in every church. This secret service, by means of prayer, will protect the pastor. For our churches to come into revival and become the group of people that God has called them to be, we must pray for our pastors.

If the statement 'everything rises and falls on leadership' is true, then when we fail to pray for our leaders, our doom is, potentially, at our own feet. It is our job to undergird our pastors and their families. It is our job to protect them from spiritual harm and to guard their interests from the one who would love to steal, kill, and destroy them.

It is time for our churches to rise up, and the first place to arise is in prayer for its spiritual leaders. Now is the time. Now is the season. Now is the moment to do the will of God. Let us not be hearers of the Word. Let us be doers.

Printed in the United States
212137BV00005B/1/P

9 781607 913481